KU-208-372

112783

POPULATION DILEMMAS
IN THE MIDDLE EAST

In memory of my father,
Herbert Silbermann

POPULATION DILEMMAS IN THE MIDDLE EAST

ESSAYS IN POLITICAL DEMOGRAPHY AND ECONOMY

GAD G. GILBAR
*University of Haifa and
Moshe Dayan Center, Tel Aviv University*

FRANK CASS
LONDON • PORTLAND, OR

First Published in 1997 in Great Britain by
FRANK CASS & CO. LTD.
Newbury House, 900 Eastern Avenue
London, IG2 7HH

and in the United States of America by
FRANK CASS
c/o ISBS, 5804 N.E. Hassalo Street
Portland, Oregon, 97213-3644

British Library Cataloguing in Publication Data:

A catalogue record for this book is available
from the British Library

ISBN 0-7146-4706-3 (cloth)
ISBN 0-7146-4244-4 (paperback)

Library of Congress Cataloging-in-Publication Data:

A catalog record for this book is available
from the Library of Congress

Printed in Great Britain by
Bookcraft (Bath) Ltd, Midsomer Norton, Avon

Contents

Tables

ix

Figures and Illustrations

Abbreviations

AAS	*Asian and African Studies*
ARE	Arab Republic of Egypt
CAPMAS	Central Agency for Public Mobilisation and Statistics (Cairo)
CBS	Central Bureau of Statistics (Jerusalem)
DESIPA	Department for Economic and Social Information and Policy Analysis
DK	Dawlat al-kuwayt
DS	Department of Statistics (Amman)
EIU	Economist Intelligence Unit
ESCWA	Economic and Social Commission for Western Asia
GDP	Gross Domestic Product
GNP	Gross National Product
HKJ	The Hashemite Kingdom of Jordan
IBRD	International Bank for Reconstruction and Development
IJMES	*International Journal of Middle East Studies*
IMF	International Monetary Fund
J'AS	al-Jumhuriyya al-'arabiyya al-suriyya
JPS	*Journal of Palestine Studies*
JSGAS	*Judaea, Samaria and Gaza Area Statistics*
MECS	*Middle East Contemporary Survey*
MEED	*Middle East Economic Digest*
MEJ	*Middle East Journal*
MENA	Middle East News Agency
MES	*Middle Eastern Studies*
MTM	*Marchés Tropicaux et Méditerranéens*

OAPEC	Organization of Arab Petroleum Exporting Countries
PE	*Petroleum Economist*
PLO	Palestine Liberation Organization
SAI	*Statistical Abstract of Israel*
SY	*Statistical Yearbook*
UNCTAD	United Nations Conference on Trade and Development
UNDP	United Nations Development Programme
UNFPA	United Nations Fund for Population Activities
UNIDO	United Nations Industrial Development Organization
UNRWA	United Nations Relief and Works Agency for Palestine Refugees in the Near East
USAID	United States Agency for International Development
WB	World Bank

Preface

For over a generation, demographic developments have had a crucial bearing on the economic, social and political situation in a number of countries in the Middle East. In the economic sphere, rapid population growth has contributed critically to multiple hardships — in employment, housing and physical and social infrastructure. It has also stunted the process of economic growth, hindered improvement in standard of living and economic well-being, and been responsible for the persistence, or worsening, of poverty. In the social sphere, rapid population growth has been one of the factors accelerating the process of urbanization, on the one hand, and external migration, mainly for purposes of employment, on the other. The effects of these processes have been felt both in the economic sphere — for example, the expansion of the non-formal economy — and in the social sphere — for example, greater integration of women into the labor force. On the political level, the most noteworthy phenomenon in this context has been the strong connection between demographic changes and the strengthening of radical Islamic organizations, their message eagerly received by considerable portions of the population.

The focus of this book are demographic developments that have occurred in two Middle Eastern societies, the Palestinian and the Egyptian, and the political implications attributable to these developments in the period from the late 1940s and early 1950s till the early 1990s, the starting point for analysis of the Palestinian society being the 1948 war, and of the Egyptian society, the 1952 revolution. More than other Islamic societies in the Middle East, the Palestinians and the Egyptians have been influenced in recent decades by demographic change, to the extent that no important area in these societies has been unaffected by population movement, that is, natural increase or migration.

The first part of the book deals with developments in Palestinian society, starting with a general outline of the process of Palestinian population growth after the exodus of 1948 until the end of 1987. During this period, a major demographic change in the history of the Palestinians took place: the creation of large Palestinian communities east of the Jordan River, especially in the Hashemite Kingdom of Jordan. Several factors, economic and political, caused changes in the absolute and relative size of the Palestinian communities, and these are discussed in Chapter 1.

The three chapters that follow detail various aspects of the Palestinian migration as well as the high rates of natural increase within the Palestinian community. Chapter 2 presents the domestic conditions in the early 1950s which impelled a growing number of Palestinians to migrate from the West Bank eastward, and focuses on the town of Nablus and the refugee camps in its environs. This town, which had enjoyed economic prosperity in the latter years of the Mandate era, faced serious difficulties after the 1948 war following its severance from the coastal plain and the influx of tens of thousands of refugees from Israel. In addition, it suffered from the policy of the Jordanian government, which concentrated its efforts on the development of the East Bank of the kingdom. One of the consequences of these developments was the start of a migratory movement to the East Bank and the oil economies of the Arabian Peninsula a few years after the annexation in 1950 of the West Bank to Jordan, which continued with growing intensity until the early 1980s.

The recession that struck the Arab oil economies in the early 1980s slowed this migratory movement, thereby shutting off the valve that afforded relief from economic pressures in the West Bank and the Gaza Strip. To add to this misfortune, the Israeli government in those years did not encourage investment in the territories. The economic crisis that resulted was one of the main factors leading to the eruption of the Intifada in December 1987. Chapter 3 analyzes demographic and economic developments in the years preceding the uprising. Significantly, the policy of restraining economic growth in the territories, first by the government of Jordan and then by the government of

Israel, played a central role in the two important demographic developments experienced by the Palestinians in the West Bank in the last two generations — the eastward migration and its cessation.

The third and final development in the field of migration in the period under review is the departure/expulsion of most of the Palestinians residing in Kuwait and their return to Jordan. About 300,000 Palestinians left Kuwait in the course of a few months following the invasion of the principality by the Iraqi army in July 1990 and the outbreak of the Gulf war in January 1991. Since most of them held Jordanian nationality, they set out for Jordan. One of the largest Palestinian communities in the Arab states was thus reabsorbed into Jordan. This increment to the kingdom's population exacerbated demographic and economic pressures existing in Jordan since the late 1980s, and was one of the factors prompting the Jordanian government to adopt a family planning policy in 1993. This antinatalist policy evolved despite misgivings in Amman and powerful political and social forces acting against it. Chapter 4, which closes the first part of the book, traces the change in Jordan's demographic policy and the influence it exerted on the demographic development of the Palestinians there.

By contrast to Palestinian society, whose demographic development was the product of a combination of high rates of natural increase and large-scale migratory movements, the balancing effect of migratory movements was limited in Egyptian society, which was forced to confront more intensively the effects of high rates of natural increase. Earlier than most societies in the Middle East, Egypt faced the prospect of demographic constraints and the need to adopt a policy slowing the rate of population growth, namely a birth control policy.

From the start, Egypt's leaders after the July 1952 revolution were aware of the grave consequences of rapid population growth, but they did not press for steps that might reduce fertility rates. Only in the mid-1960s, did Nasser adopt a family planning policy. Chapter 5 unfolds the first stage of Egypt's antinatalist policy, points out the factors involved in the prolonged postponement of these first steps, and examines the effectiveness of governmental activity in this area during the last year of Nasser's leadership.

Under Sadat, the government withdrew from a direct antinatalist policy. Egypt put its faith in accelerated and comprehensive economic change after the 1973 war, hoping that it would result in a large-scale flow of capital into the Egyptian economy. Where Nasser had striven to release Egyptian society from its distress through intensive government intervention in economic activity, and particularly by initiating large-scale state investment in the economy, Sadat was confident that the opening of the economy to foreign and domestic investors would renew the growth process and bring about a revival of the economy and society. This would, by itself, lead to a reduction in the rates of population growth, without the need for intervention by the government. In particular, Sadat believed that the Arab oil states, primarily Saudi Arabia, would channel a substantial flow of capital into the reconstruction of the Egyptian economy following the 1973 war. On the face of it, this expectation could not have been more natural: the Arab states which were rich in capital and poor in human resources would aid the Arab state which was the most populous but poor in other resources. Chapter 6 scrutinizes Sadat's recipe, showing why it proved illusory and eventually pushed the Egyptian president to seek other solutions. These in turn led not only to a change in Egypt's economic system but to the opening of a new era in Israeli-Arab relations.

In fact, only in the mid-1980s, over thirty years after the leaders of Egypt recognized the existence of a demographic problem, did a policy take shape that resolutely sought to achieve real results. This policy, initiated by Mubarak in 1985, aimed to create a public atmosphere supporting birth control, while at the same time making contraceptives available to the many couples who wished to practice family planning. Within a few years, the policy produced notable results. A significant decline in the natural increase rate was noted and population growth, which had increased yearly, was stemmed. Family planning policy in Egypt was unique in that it generated remarkable results without recourse to stick-and-carrot measures, that is, without coercion and without inducements. Chapter 7 covers the various aspects of Mubarak's family planning policy from 1985 to 1992.

By the end of 1993, the two societies, Palestinian and Egyptian, had each concluded a long chapter in their demographic development and each faced a new departure. The Oslo accords signed in September 1993 between Israel and the PLO were intended to initiate fresh processes, especially in an area central to the Palestinians — the sphere of migration and relations between the large communities of the West Bank and the Gaza Strip on the one hand, and Jordan, Lebanon and Syria on the other. In the case of Egypt, government and society had successfully met the challenge of implementing a family planning policy, which just a few years earlier had appeared hopeless. It had accelerated the process of lowering fertility and natural increase rates to the point of an anticipated halt in the absolute growth of the population as early as the coming decade.

Five chapters in this book were published previously in slightly different form. Chapter 2 originally appeared as "The Economy of Nablus and the Hashemites: The Early Years, 1949-56" in *Middle Eastern Studies* 5/1 (1989): 51-63. It is reprinted here by permission of Frank Cass. An earlier version of Chapter 5 was published as "Egypt from Laissez-Faire to 'Soft Revolution': Birthrates, Saving Patterns, and Economic Growth" in Shimon Shamir (ed.), *Egypt from Monarchy to Republic*, Boulder: Westview Press, 1995, pp. 66-80. It is reprinted by permission of Westview Press. Chapter 6 was initially published as "Wealth, Want, and Arab Unity: Saudi-Egyptian Relations, 1962-1985" in *The Jerusalem Journal of International Relations* 9/3 (1987): 65-84. It is reprinted by permission of the Johns Hopkins University Press. Finally, chapters 7 and 4 first appeared in *The Middle East Contemporary Survey* 16 (1992): 335-48, and 17 (1993): 262-70. They are reprinted by permission of the Moshe Dayan Center for Middle Eastern and African Studies, Tel Aviv University.

I have been fortunate in receiving the help of friends and colleagues who have made useful comments on various chapters of the book. I am grateful to Mohammad L. Ali, Ami Ayalon, Erhard Franz, Samir Hazboun, Uri M. Kupferschmidt, Itamar Rabinovich, Shimon Shamir and Asher Susser. I am also sincerely thankful to Judy Krausz, Dick Bruggeman, Zehava Hava, Shlomit Shehnik, Murray Rosovsky and Onn Winckler for their assistance at various stages of the research and in the preparation of the manuscript, and to Iris Fruchter, who took care of the index. I am deeply indebted to the librarians at the Cairo Demographic Center, the Dayan Center Library, the Middle East Documentation Unit at Durham University Library and the University of Haifa Library. Finally, my research on Palestinian and Egyptian demographic development was generously supported by the Dayan Center – Tel Aviv University, the University of Haifa's Research Authority, and the German-Israeli Foundation for Scientific Research and Development (GIF).

Introduction

The Policies of Demographic Change

NATAL POLICIES: CONTROL VS. ENCOURAGEMENT

The relationship between demographic development and political response manifests itself in a number of ways and can thus be studied from various angles. The following discussion deals mainly with the impact of political decisions on demographic development in Middle Eastern countries during the twentieth century and looks at primarily two areas: (1) political intervention vis-à-vis fertility and natural increase, and (2) political decisions and actions regarding mass migratory movements. Focus is on direct political influence only, i.e., on those decisions governments take so as to instigate demographic change, with secondary effects left out of the discussion.

Rulers and governments of most Middle Eastern countries have tried to influence the rates of natural increase of their populations. Their motivations for intervening and attempting to affect fertility were varied. Generally speaking, the states in which governments were active in influencing family size may be divided into two main groups:

(1)   States in which the government sought to bring about a drop in the rates of natural increase by motivating couples within the fertile age range to adopt the idea of family planning and content themselves with a small number of children (generally two to four). In the early 1990s this group included Tunisia, Turkey, Egypt, Iran, Morocco and Algeria.

(2)   States whose rulers or governments sought to raise the

rates of natural increase by encouraging couples within the fertile age range to have more children than they had wanted or planned. The group that maintained a policy of encouraging high fertility rates included Saudi Arabia, Kuwait, Libya, the United Arab Emirates, Iran, Iraq and Israel.

The inclusion of Iran in both groups is no error, as the rulers of Iran adopted contrary natal policies in different periods. A family planning policy was adopted during the last phase of the Pahlavi regime in 1966–78 and reintroduced at the end of 1988 by the Islamic Republic.[1] The decade between these two periods (1979–88) witnessed a rejection of the family planning policy by Ayatollah Khomeyni, who advocated a pronatalist policy.[2]

The states not included in the two groups mentioned above — Jordan, Syria, Lebanon, Yemen and Sudan — announced the adoption of family planning policies during the 1970s, but activities undertaken in the direction of birth control were limited.

The difference in natal policy between the first group of states and the second reflects the differing political, economic and social conditions in the countries involved. In the first group, the political elites in each of these countries had come to the conclusion that their societies suffered from an overpopulation syndrome, namely, that high rates of natural increase were a primary factor in delaying the attainment of rapid economic growth. Egypt, Turkey, Iran and Morocco were prime examples of countries caught in the syndrome of population pressure on economic resources during the 1960s and 1970s, as illustrated by high rates of open as well as disguised unemployment, a severe shortage of housing and the creation of urban slums inhabited by millions of rural migrants, and inadequate services.[3] Added to these domestic factors were external causes which also prompted the adoption of antinatalist policies. Starting in the 1960s, Western governments (especially the United States) and international institutions (especially the United Nations) applied pressure combined with economic aid and expertise aimed at inculcating birth control policies. All these factors account for the adoption of family planning policies during the 1960s and early 1970s. Tunisia was the first to announce the application of a birth control policy in 1964; Egypt and Turkey began implementation in 1965; Morocco and Iran in 1966; and Algeria in 1971.[4]

The political elites in these countries, in implementing family planning policies, aimed at achieving two main goals: first, arousing public awareness, especially on the part of couples in

2

the fertile age range, regarding the advantages of birth control and of having a small family for the woman as well as for the other members of the family. Emphasis was put on the advantages in terms of the woman's health and the economic wellbeing of the family. Simultaneously, efforts were made to convince the population of the anticipated advantages for society as a whole once a significant drop in rates of natural increase was obtained. The second goal was expanding the use of contraceptives by husbands and wives, especially among the rural population.

The main governmental effort was carried out by means of a wide-ranging information campaign utilizing the media, followed up by the distribution of contraceptives at a nominal price or free at mother and child clinics, family planning centers, pharmacies and private clinics.

The authorities in all of the above-mentioned countries made special efforts to obtain the support of prominent religious leaders for their family planning policy. Confirmation by distinguished 'ulama that the policy did not contradict the shari'a was considered by the authorities in all the countries in question, including Turkey, as essential to the success of the program. Another important element common to all the Islamic countries that adopted antinatalist policies was the purely voluntary character of the program, i.e., inculcation by persuasion as to the necessity of, and the benefits to be derived from, the program for the individual and for society at large. With few exceptions, policy did not include material compensation for those who responded to the appeal to raise small families. Neither did the program lean toward imposing economic or social sanctions against those who did not respond positively to achieving the goal. In other words, implementation of the policy was soft.

An explicit criterion for measuring the effect of family planning policy is the change that occurs in the rates of women of fertile age who use contraceptives regularly. Another measurement is changes in fertility rates over a period of time. The difficulty in relying on these criteria in order to assess the effect of family planning in practice, however, is that these changes are the result of many factors, only one of which — and not necessarily the decisive one — is the implementation of family planning policy. Nevertheless, research aimed at isolating the effect of antinatalist policy found that it was a highly important factor in the decision made by women, or by both partners, to adopt the idea of a small family and use contraceptives regularly over a long term.[5] For

3

example, the drop in total fertility rates that occurred in Egypt from 6.8 children in 1965 to 4.0 children in 1990 is attributable, inter alia, to the fact that the proportion of couples using contraceptives rose during 1960–90 from 10 percent to 48 percent.[6] This rise in the use of contraceptives is attributable above all to various activities undertaken by the Egyptian government in the context of its family planning policy — primarily the creation of convenient access to, and cheap availability of, contraceptive means throughout Egypt, including the rural areas.

Not coincidentally, all the Islamic states in the Middle East that adopted a pronatalist policy during the last generation belong to the group of large oil exporters in the region. These countries experienced a sharp change in their economic situation as a result of the oil-price revolution of 1973 when hundreds of millions of dollars flowed into their economies during the "oil decade" (1973–82). At the very start of the decade, a situation that could be described as a "resource pressure on population" was created — a kind of reverse situation of the demographic pressure syndrome ("population pressure on resources"). This syndrome was manifested in many ways in the major Arab oil states — Saudi Arabia, Kuwait, the United Arab Emirates and Libya — an important effect being large-scale over-demand for manpower in many areas and on various levels of expertise. The gates of these countries were opened wide to foreign workers, and although entry was on a temporary basis — entry and employment permits were granted for a few years only — this restriction did not prevent rapid growth of the foreign population in every country under discussion. Inasmuch as substantial communities of foreigners had existed in these countries even before the start of the oil decade, the new situation led not only to a considerable increase in the number of foreigners, but to foreigners accounting for over half the population in some countries. This development was particularly pronounced in, although not limited to, Kuwait: the local population (Kuwaiti citizens) in the 1980s, according to reliable estimates, constituted 35–45 percent of the total population. A 1985 census showed only 682,000 Kuwaiti citizens in a total population of 1.9 million.[7] In Saudi Arabia, although the situation did not reach the point where the local population constituted a numerical minority in its native land, during the 1980s the foreign population grew in absolute terms to a total of 4.0–4.5 million[8] — the largest foreign community in absolute terms in any Arab country.

The presence of such — also proportionally — large communities of foreigners harbored both a latent and an apparent threat to political stability in these countries. Furthermore, the dependence on a high proportion of foreign manpower was undesirable. There were two ways that the governments of these states could reduce the proportion of foreigners in the population: (1) granting full citizenship to large groups of foreigners who had been resident for prolonged periods; and (2) creating conditions that would encourage a high birthrate within the local population. The first option was rejected by all the oil states under discussion, leaving only the adoption of pronatalist policies.

The three other countries that also adopted policies encouraging a high birthrate during certain periods — Iran, Iraq and Israel — were motivated by other factors. If the oil states were propelled primarily by domestic factors, the three countries in question adopted pronatalist policies in light of an external threat, namely, prolonged external conflicts that created a strong demand for local manpower. The adoption of pronatalist policies in Iran and Iraq developed in light of a bitter war with numerous casualties that lasted some eight years, while in Israel the question of the size of the Jewish population was viewed by many as vitally related to the ability of the Jewish state to survive in the prolonged conflict with its Arab neighbors.

In applying pronatalist policies, governments and rulers acted to inculcate the importance of achieving the desired goals within the various sectors of the population, as well as to create conditions conducive to raising fertility rates. The element of persuasion through the media, however, was marginal. Few encouraging statements were made, and, with minor exceptions, the approach to the population was not direct or blunt.[9] Moreover, it would appear that the broader the application of the practical — economic — element of the policy, in terms of a support basket granted to broad sectors of the population, the less frequent the resort to admonition and exhortation along the lines, for example, of Saddam Husayn's rebuke of Iraq's women in 1986 for shirking their duty to produce children.[10] The emphasis in the oil states, by contrast, was on creating conditions that would encourage couples in the fertile age range to have a large number of children (eight or more).[11] Kuwait and Saudi Arabia in particular were able to allocate considerable resources to promoting this policy.

5

POLITICS AND MIGRATION

The countries of the Middle East witnessed several population migrations during the twentieth century, some of them motivated by economic and social developments such as the migration of Egyptian, Jordanian, Syrian and other workers to the oil states. This kind of migration will not be dealt with here, but rather the focus will be on the waves of migration that were impelled by political developments or that were the byproduct of political decisions. Although the distinction between "economic" and "political" migrations is not always clear, it is on the whole possible, nevertheless, to distinguish between these two types of population movements in the history of the region.

The waves of migration that had a political background can be classified according to the positions or approaches adopted by each of three elements integral in them: the government of the country of origin, the government of the country of destination, and the migrant population itself.

Migratory movements termed population exchanges should also be mentioned. These population movements are typified by their two-way nature: migratory movements between two or more countries take place simultaneously, with each country serving as a country of origin, a destination, or both. Customarily, a distinction is made between voluntary population exchange movements (i.e., the populations involved migrate of their own free will) and forced population exchanges. Another distinction is between "arranged" population exchanges (i.e., involving cooperation between the governments of the countries of origin and destination) and "non-arranged" population exchange movements.

An instructive example of interaction between political forces and the occurrence of a migratory wave — the largest in the history of the Middle East during the twentieth century — is the population exchange between Turkey and Greece. The accepted version of the event is that the population exchange that took place between Turkey and Greece during 1923–25, when some 1.7 million people migrated from their birthplace and homes, is an example of an arranged and voluntary population exchange procedure between two countries that had been in a bitter war with each other shortly beforehand. In fact, the development of events was far from being the result of advance planning or voluntary movement on the part of either of the populations.

The migration had its roots in the pre-First World War period

6

when during the Balkan War (1912–13) Greece occupied several Aegean islands off the Anatolian coast — Lemnos, Mytilene, Chios and others. This caused deep apprehension on the part of the Young Turks, the rulers of the Ottoman Empire, who feared that Greece would establish protection over the Greek communities (i.e., Greek Orthodox by religion) in Anatolia itself. These fears were not unfounded: the idea of unifying all the territories inhabited by Greeks into a single sovereign entity gained ascendancy in Greece at that time. In light of these developments, the Young Turks proposed a population exchange to the Greek government, similar to an arrangement they had made with the Bulgarian government at that time. The proposal envisioned the transfer of the Greek population living along the Aegean coast to territories under Greek sovereignty, and the transfer of the Muslim population living within Greek boundaries to territories under Ottoman control.

At first, the Greek government showed no interest in the Ottoman proposal, whereupon the Ottomans ordered the exile of the Greek population from the Aegean coast and Anatolian territory. By early 1914, the Ottomans had exiled 150,000 Greek inhabitants from the coast of Asia Minor to territories under Greek control, and an additional 50,000 to areas in the interior of Anatolia. At that point, the Greek government was prepared to enter discussions and a mixed Ottoman-Greek commission convened in Izmir in June 1914 to consider an exchange proposal whereby the Greek population residing in the Izmir region and in Thrace would move to Greece, and the Muslim population residing in Greek Macedonia would migrate to Ottoman Anatolia. Two months after the commission convened, the Ottoman Empire entered the war (August 1914) and the work of the commission was halted before it could formulate detailed recommendations.

With the end of the First World War, the Greeks again raised the idea of a population exchange, but meanwhile Anatolia and Thrace underwent a tumultuous and fateful period that fundamentally changed the situation of the minorities involved, i.e., the Greeks in Turkey and the Muslims in Greece. Basing themselves on agreements between Britain and Greece concluded during the war, large Greek forces invaded the Izmir region in May 1919 and in the course of a year, by the summer of 1920, conquered sizable areas in western Anatolia. Turkish forces launched a counterattack in August 1922 and by September retook all of Anatolia. An armistice signed on 10 October in Mudanya recognized Turkish sovereignty in Anatolia and in eastern Thrace. What is relevant to the present discussion is the fact that with the withdrawal in the summer of 1922 of the Greek forces from the territories that Greece had conquered or controlled in Anatolia and eastern Thrace, a mass flight of the Greek population began, prompted by fear of the advancing army under Mustafa Kemal Atatürk. Estimates put the number of Greek refugees who abandoned their homes in the summer of 1922 at one million. Discussions were subsequently held between Turkish and Greek representatives during the final months of 1922 over the fate of the refugees, culminating in the Lausanne Agreement signed by both sides on 30 January 1923 which established a population exchange between the two countries. Paragraph 1 of the agreement stated explicitly that what was envisioned was a compulsory exchange, with no possibility for the populations involved to return to their place of origin at any time in the future.

During 1923–25 (and primarily during May–October 1924), 188,000 Greek Orthodox inhabitants moved from Turkey to Greece, and 355,000 Muslims moved from Greece to Turkey. Numerous problems relating to property rights in the territories that had been abandoned and to compensation payments were dealt with by the Ankara Agreement signed in June 1930, although in practice none of the refugees on either side received real compensation for property left behind.[12]

The agreed population exchange, therefore, did not involve 1.7 million people, but a smaller number — 543,000 people; it was not a voluntary exchange but a forced exchange; and, most importantly, it was an exchange that followed a bitter war between two countries and was a product of it. The million Greek refugees had expected a solution to their situation of distress with the signing of the armistice of 1922, but Atatürk adamantly refused to return them to their homes, and managed to obtain the support of the powers, especially Britain, for his position. The Greek government had no choice, in this situation, but to agree to the exchange. The motivation for the evacuation of the Muslim Turkish population was purely to ease absorption and settlement arrangements for the Greek war refugees. What emerges, therefore, was that the Lausanne Agreement was not an agreement for a population exchange, but an agreement for the settlement of a million Greek refugees who had fled in the summer of 1922 from territories in Greece conquered by the Turkish army. This was, in fact, how the agreement was viewed by the Greek prime minister, Eleftherio Venizelos, who observed, in July 1923: "The exile of the population from Asia Minor did not result from the exchange agreement, but was a fait accompli in which [in accordance with the terms of the Lausanne Agreement] I simply received Turkey's agreement to evacuate the Muslim Turks from Greece in order to aid the resettlement of the Greek refugees."[13]

CONCLUSION

What can be learned from these events and episodes in which rulers and governments sought to influence demographic developments in their countries? First, the attempts by rulers and governments in the Middle Eastern countries to influence fertility rates elicited complex results, inasmuch as other factors besides natal policy affected fertility rates as well. Although some of these factors were related to government-initiated activity (e.g., the expansion of secondary and higher education systems and the admission into them of growing numbers of students, or induced activity to expand employment opportunities for women), they were not formulated as part of, or as the application of, a demographic policy. Furthermore, three pronounced characteristics of demographic policies in the Middle East are discernible:

(1) Natalist policy was granted higher priority in those countries that were most acutely affected by increased population pressure on available resources. Thus, natal policy played a more central role in governmental activity in countries that advocated birth control than in those that encouraged high fertility.

(2) Diversified and prolonged governmental efforts to apply birth control policies produced results. This was true especially for Egypt during the late 1980s and early 1990s, when a drop in total fertility rates and birthrates was recorded. While many factors unrelated to the application of family planning policies contributed to this development, it would appear that the various steps taken by the government in this area did have a significant effect on the drop in fertility rates and birthrates.

(3) Intervention by rulers and governments in propelling mass migratory movements was effective in situations of exceptional political and military circumstances. Rulers in most cases did not have to instigate the exile of local inhabitants from their homes, but once a mass flight of civilians began during the course of war, the dynamic that developed soon turned into policy.

9

Notes

1. On the reintroduction of family planning policy in Iran in the late 1980s, see Nesta Ramazani, "Women in Iran: The Revolutionary Ebb and Flow," *MEJ* 47/3 (1993): 414–16; Homa Hoodfar, "Devices and Desires," *Middle East Report* 24/5 (1994): 12–14.
2. See Yasmin L. Mossavar-Rahmani, "Family Planning in Post-Revolutionary Iran," in Guity Nashat (ed.), *Women and Revolution in Iran*, Boulder: Westview Press, 1983, p. 257.
3. On population pressure in Egypt, see, e.g. *al-Ahram al-Iqtisadi*, 6 July 1992; on the demographic distress in Iran, see *Kayhan*, 11 July 1993.
4. WB, *Population Change and Economic Development*, New York: Oxford University Press, 1985, pp. 160–61, table 6.
5. UN, Department of International Economic and Social Affairs, *Studies to Enhance the Evaluation of Family Planning Programmes*, New York: UN, 1985, pp. 180, 199, 218–19.
6. See below, pp. 114–15, 117.
7. DK, al-Idara al-markaziyya lil-ihsa'a, *al-Majmu'a al-ihsa'iyya al-sanawiyya*, 1985 (hereafter: *MIS*). See also *MEED*, 16 May 1987, p. 47.
8. *MEED*, 23 May 1987, p. 37.
9. See, e.g., statement by the Kuwaiti Minister for Planning in *al-Ra'y al-'Amm*, 5 August 1989.
10. *al-Jumhuriyya* (Baghdad), 4 May 1986.
11. UN, Department of International Economic and Social Affairs, *World Population Policies*, vol. 3, New York: UN, 1990, p. 80; Baquer Salman al-Najjar, "Population Policies in the Countries of the Gulf Co-operation Council: Politics and Society," *Immigrants and Minorities* 12 (1993): 211–12.
12. For a detailed description, see Stephan P. Ladas, *The Exchange of Minorities. Bulgaria, Greece and Turkey*, New York: Macmillan, 1932, pp. 567–83; Harry J. Psomiades, *The Eastern Question: The Last Phase*, Thessaloniki: Institute for Balkan Studies, 1968, pp. 60–68.
13. Psomiades, p. 65.

1

Population Growth and Migration: The Palestinian Communities, 1949–87

INTRODUCTION

One of the major consequences of the 1948 war was the demographic displacement thrust upon the Palestinian population in the territory that had made up Mandatory Palestine. By the end of 1948 approximately half of them had abandoned their homes, whether of their own accord or as a result of actions by Jewish forces. The figures for refugees and their whereabouts at the war's end, however, are all estimates, only a few of which are based on information originating in the refugee camps.[1] There are no well-founded data on the Palestinian dispersion at the beginning of 1949, and it is doubtful if such data can ever be compiled. The most reasonable estimate is that 630,000–670,000 people left their homes during 1948. Of these, about 360,000–380,000 moved to the West Bank and Gaza Strip and about 240,000 crossed into the three neighboring Arab states of Lebanon, Transjordan and Syria (see table 1.1).

In 1949, after the war had ended and the last of the armistice agreements had been signed, the Palestinian population (permanent inhabitants and refugees) numbered about 1.316 million people, scattered over six areas or states. The largest concentration, about 670,000, was in the West Bank, accounting for about half of the total Palestinian population that year. The second largest concentration, about 240,000, was in the Gaza Strip, and the third, some 146,000, remained in the State of Israel. Thus, in 1949 about 80 percent of the total Palestinian population (over one million people) lived within the formen boundaries of Mandatory Palestine. The next three largest concentrations were located in neighboring Arab states: Lebanon — about 100,000; Transjordan — 70,000-80,000; and Syria — about 70,000 (see table 1.1). A few thousand Palestinians went to other Arab countries, primarily Egypt and Iraq.[2] Notably, the Palestinians who crossed into Transjordan in 1949 constituted only about 5 percent of the total Palestinian population, and no more than about 18 percent of the total population of Transjordan.[3]

Two demographic trends within the Palestinian population stood out during the course of the 39 years from the end of the war in 1949 until the onset of the Intifada at the end of 1987. The first was continued rapid population growth in both absolute and relative terms. While high rates of natural increase characterized the Palestinian Arab population in the Mandate period, these rates were unprecedentedly high during the period under study, and in comparison with other Islamic societies in the Middle East as well. The second trend, essentially a result of

Table 1.1

The Palestinians: population estimates by place of residence, 1949 and 1987
(end of year)

	1949		1987	
	thousands	percent	thousands	percent
Israel	146	11	718	16
West Bank	670	51	860	19
Gaza Strip	240	18	564	12
Jordan	70	5	1,200	26
Lebanon	100	8	270	6
Syria	70	5	240	5
Kuwait	—		300	7
Saudi Arabia, UAE, Oman, Qatar, Bahrain	—		200	4
Other countries	20	2	250	5
Total	1,316	100	4,602	100

Sources: See text.

12

Figure 1.1
The Palestinians: population estimates by place of residence
1949 and 1987

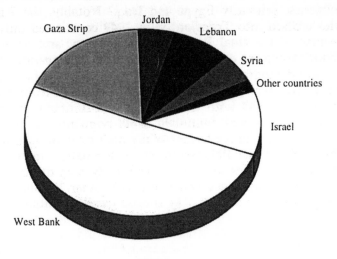

1949

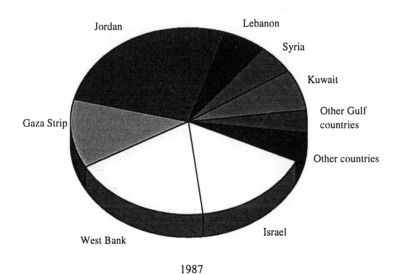

1987

Source: table 1.1

13

the demographic, economic and political changes of 1948–49, was the movement of the Palestinian population from one region to another, or from one Arab state to another, especially from the West Bank to states east of the Jordan River.

A detailed discussion of these two trends is not possible, because none of the states with a substantial Palestinian population, with the exception of Israel, has systematically collected demographic data for that community during the entire period. From the 1967 war onward, the populations in the West Bank and the Gaza Strip were covered by a separate Israeli statistical survey initiated in September 1967 by the Central Bureau of Statistics (CBS). At that time, the CBS conducted a census in the territories and has since been publishing demographic data on a wide range of subjects, including rate of natural increase, balance of migration, and distribution of the population by sex, age and education.[4] The CBS data on the West Bank and the Gaza Strip are considered reliable and are used, generally without reservation, by Israeli and Palestinian experts alike (including the authors of Palestine Liberation Organization [PLO] statistical publications),[5] as well as other researchers. Nevertheless, there are indications that the 1967 census suffered from undercounting.[6] Inasmuch as there has been no other census since 1967, these errors have not been corrected and have influenced all estimates extrapolated from them.

Regarding the other Palestinian communities, including the major ones in Jordan and Lebanon, there has been no comprehensive or consistent collection of data for political reasons, and researchers must make do with estimates (usually rough) and educated guesses. Clearly, in such circumstances, considerations unrelated to academic research may have been at work shifting figures up or down to serve vested interests. It must be emphasized, therefore, that regarding aggregate data on the Palestinian population through the end of 1987, including communities in Arab states, only estimates are available, which for all the close examination and scrutiny they may undergo, remain only that.

NATURAL INCREASE

On the basis of existing estimates, it would appear that at the end of 1987 the total Palestinian population was about 4.6 million. According to this estimate, the Palestinian population increased by 256 percent (from 1.294 million at the end of 1947 to 4.602 million at the end of 1987), representing an average annual growth rate of 3.2 percent.[7] This rate of growth was substantially higher than growth rates during the first half of the century (see table 1.2). Hence, while in the four decades prior to the 1948 war the Palestinian population grew by 750,000–800,000, in the four decades following it the population grew by 3.3 million.

The rise in the natural increase rates, and their sustained high level, account for the growth of the Palestinian population. However, complete data on natural increase rates throughout the period under study are available only for the Palestinian Arab population in Israel. These rates were constant at about 30 per thousand during the first half of the 1940s and then climbed during the next twenty years, peaking at an average annual growth rate of 43.5 per thousand in 1961–65. Since then there has been a clear downward trend, with a drop to 29 per thousand in 1984–87.[8]

The natural increase rates of the Arab population in Israel during the period under review are high even in comparison with other Middle Eastern Islamic societies. Table 1.3 provides data on natural increase rates during the period 1960–80 in six states (Turkey, Egypt, Iran, Iraq, Syria and Jordan) for which reasonably reliable figures are available (albeit within fairly wide margins). The data show the extent to which natural increase

Table 1.2

The Palestinians: population growth and natural increase rates, 1870–1947

Population growth (in thousands)	
1870	350
1914	600
1947	1,294
Natural increase rates (per thousand)[a]	
1922–25	23.3
1926–30	25.2
1931–35	25.0
1936–40	27.6
1941–45	32.1

Note: a Muslim population only.
Sources: Gad Gilbar, "Megamot ba-hitpathut ha-demographit shel 'arviyei' eretz-yisrael, 1870–1948," *Cathedra* 45 (1987): 46–47, tables 2 and 3.

Table 1.3
Six Middle Eastern states: birthrate, death rate and natural
increase rate, 1960-80 (various years)
(per thousand)

		1960	1965	1970	1975	1980
Turkey						
	BR	43.1	41.2	37.9	33.6	32.9
	DR	15.8	14.4	12.2	10.4	9.5
	NIR	27.3	26.8	25.7	23.2	23.4
Egypt						
	BR	43.5	41.7	38.5	37.6	36.6
	DR	19.0	17.0	15.1	13.6	12.1
	NIR	24.5	24.7	23.4	24.0	24.5
Iran						
	BR	45.5	44.4	43.3	42.5	42.6
	DR	17.4	15.2	13.2	11.7	11.1
	NIR	28.1	29.2	30.1	30.8	31.5
Iraq						
	BR	49.4	49.1	48.1	47.2	47.0
	DR	19.9	17.9	15.8	13.8	12.4
	NIR	29.5	31.2	32.3	33.4	33.6
Syria						
	BR	47.0	47.5	46.5	45.9	47.1
	DR	17.7	16.0	13.5	10.3	8.1
	NIR	29.3	31.5	33.0	35.6	39.0
Jordan						
	BR	47.4	48.0	47.6	47.0	46.6
	DR	19.9	17.5	15.5	12.6	9.4
	NIR	27.5	30.5	32.1	34.4	37.2

Note:
BR = Birthrate
DR = Death Rate
NIR = Natural increase Rate
Source: WB, *World Tables*, 1983, pp. 28, 44, 45, 49, 87, 93.

rates of the Arabs in Israel exceeded those of neighboring Islamic societies, a situation that was especially pronounced in the 1960s. These data do not, however, show the significant difference in natural increase rates between the two Arab communities in Israel, Muslim and Christian. The natural increase rates of the Muslim population continued to rise until the mid-1960s, with a downward trend appearing only toward the end of the decade, while they declined in the Christian Arab population beginning in the early 1950s and possibly before, a trend that persisted until the mid-1980s. The rise in growth rates within the Muslim community during the first part of the period under study was particularly sharp (see table 1.4), resulting in a wide gap in natural increase rates between the two communities. At its peak during certain years in the 1960s and 1970s, this gap reached 23 per thousand, and accounts for the considerable shift in the numerical balance of the two Palestinian Arab communities in Israel. At the end of 1949 Muslims constituted 76.6 percent of the total Arab population; by the end of 1987 their relative share had risen to 85.6 percent. The proportion of Christians fell accordingly, from 23.4 percent in 1949 to only 14.4 percent in 1987. In absolute terms, the size of the Muslim population increased from 111,500 at the end of 1949 to about 500,000 at the end of 1987 (excluding the residents of East Jerusalem), representing a 4.5-fold increase,

Table 1.4

Israel: natural increase rates of the Arab population, by religion, 1953-87
(per thousand)

	Muslims	Christians
1953–54	40.9	24.2
1955–59	38.3	27.1
1960–64	45.3	28.0
1965–69	44.9	24.5
1970–74	43.7	19.9
1975–79	39.5	18.2
1980–84	33.6	14.5
1985–87	30.9	15.5

Sources:
1953   CBS, *SAI 1954*, p. 15, table 12.
1954   id., *SAI 1960*, p. 33, table 2.
1955–87 id., *SAI 1989*, pp. 103–4, table 3/1.

while the Christian population increased during those years from 34,000 to about 86,000 (excluding East Jerusalem), or a 2.5-fold increase (see table 1.5).

The primary factor in the rise in natural increase rates of the Muslim population was a decline in mortality rates. Death rates fell to as low as 6.4 per thousand in the late 1960s, and 3.4 per thousand in 1986–87. Birthrates continued to be high in the first part of the period under study, with even a registered rise in birthrates in the first half of the 1960s. However, the birthrate began to fall off fairly rapidly from the end of the 1960s until it stood at 34 per thousand in 1986–87.[9] The average natural increase rate of the Muslim population between 1953 and 1987 was 42.2 per thousand.

In order to get some idea of the extent to which these trends in the rate of natural increase of the Muslims in Israel reflect those of the Palestinian population at large, the data above may be compared with those of the only two other Palestinian communities for which such material has been published: the West Bank and Gaza. According to population estimates published by the CBS since September 1967 (see table 1.6), the natural

Table 1.5
Israel: Arab population by religion, 1950-87
(in thousands)

End of year	Muslims	Christians	Druze[c]	Total
1950	116.1	36.0	15.0	167.1
1955	136.3	43.3	19.0	198.6
1960	166.3	49.6	23.3	239.2
1965	212.4	57.1	29.8	299.3
1970[a]	328.6	75.5	35.9	440.0
1975	411.4	80.2	42.2	533.8
1980	498.3	89.9	50.7	638.9
1985[b]	577.6	99.4	72.0	749.0
1987	617.5	103.0	76.1	793.6

Notes:
a From 1970 onward, including the Arab population of East Jerusalem.
b From 1982 onward, including the Druze and Muslim populations of the Golan sub-district.
c Including "others."
Source: CBS, *SAI 1988*, p. 31, table 2/1.

18

Table 1.6

West Bank and Gaza Strip: population estimates, 1968-87

	West Bank		Gaza Strip	
End of year	Total population (thousands)	Annual growth (percent)	Total population (thousands)	Annual growth (percent)
1968	583.1	-0.5	356.8	-6.3
1969	597.9	2.5	363.9	2.0
1970	607.8	1.7	370.0	1.7
1971	622.6	2.4	378.8	2.4
1972	633.5	1.8	387.0	2.2
1973	652.4	3.0	401.5	3.7
1974	669.7	2.7	414.0	3.1
1975	675.2	0.8	425.5	2.8
1976	683.3	1.2	437.4	2.8
1977	695.7	1.8	450.8	3.1
1978	708.0	1.8	463.0	2.7
1979	718.6	1.5	444.7	2.5
1980	724.3	0.8	456.5	2.7
1981	731.8	1.0	468.9	2.7
1982	749.3	2.4	477.3	1.8
1983	771.8	3.0	494.5	3.6
1984	793.4	2.8	509.9	3.1
1985	815.5	2.8	527.0	3.4
1986	837.7	2.7	545.0	3.4
1987	868.1	3.6	565.6	3.8

Source: CBS, *SAI 1989*, p. 700, table 27/1.

increase rate of the entire Palestinian population in the West Bank (permanent inhabitants and refugees) was about 29 per thousand in the early 1970s (1971-73). During the following 15 years, this rate showed a gradual upward trend: in the mid-1970s the average annual rate was about 30 per thousand, and in the mid-1980s about 34 per thousand. Natural increase rates during the 1968-86 period tended upward in the Gaza Strip too, and from the early 1970s they exceeded those for the West Bank, increasing from an average annual rate of about 31 per thousand in the early 1970s to about 40 per thousand in 1984-86 (see table 1.7). The average natural increase rate for 1968-86 was 30.5 per thousand in the West Bank and 34.6 per thousand in the Gaza Strip.[10]

Table 1.7
West Bank and Gaza Strip: sources of population growth, 1968-87

	Natural increase (per thousand)		Balance of population movement (in thousands)	
	West Bank	Gaza Strip	West Bank	Gaza Strip
1968	22.2	22.5	-15.8	-32.3
1969	22.9	27.8	1.3	-2.9
1970	24.7	25.6	-5.0	-3.3
1971	27.8	29.9	-2.5	-2.4
1972	28.8	31.9	-7.3	-4.0
1973	29.1	32.5	0.3	1.7
1974	32.9	35.1	-2.8	-1.8
1975	30.6	35.7	-15.1	-3.5
1976	33.1	37.3	-14.4	-4.2
1977	32.9	36.7	-10.2	-2.9
1978	30.8	37.0	-9.4	-4.7
1979	32.7	36.4	-12.6	-4.8
1980	31.7	37.5	-17.3	-5.1
1981	31.9	38.3	-15.7	-5.3
1982	33.1	37.6	-7.9	-3.1
1983	33.1	37.5	-2.7	-1.0
1984	35.0	40.2	-5.8	-4.8
1985	33.7	38.4	-5.0	-2.9
1986	33.3	40.3	-5.1	-3.6
1987	34.8	42.5	0.7	-3.3

Source: Based on CBS figures: *SAI 1989*, p. 700, table 27/1.

Demographic developments within the West Bank and Gaza Strip populations followed those of the Arabs in Israel. There is a delay of about two generations between developments in the Christian Arab population in Israel and developments in the territories, and a delay of about a single generation between Christian Arab and Muslim Arab developments in Israel. While the birthrate for Christian Arabs in Israel fell from the 1940s onward, and among Muslims from the late 1960s onward, a drop in the birthrate in the West Bank occurred only in the early 1980s, and in the Gaza Strip not until the late 1980s. Similarly, death rates declined in all four populations under discussion at widely divergent rates: a death rate of about 8-9 per thousand was registered among Christian Arabs in Israel as early as the

20

late 1940s, while similar rates were recorded among Muslims only in the latter 1950s, and in the West Bank and the Gaza Strip not until the 1980s.

Of the five Arab states with fairly large concentrations of Palestinians, only Syria published ongoing data, from the 1960s, on births and deaths of the Palestinian refugees within its territory.[11] Syria was also the only Arab state to include data on the total size of the "Registered Palestinian Refugees" (al-laji'un al-filastiniyyun al-musajjalun) in the country in its statistical yearbook (see table 1.8). These figures were in fact United Nations Relief and Works Agency (UNRWA) data. Over the years, UNRWA has published data on population size in the Palestinian refugee camps and on the natural increase rates of these populations.[12] It has long been recognized, however, that UNRWA data cannot be regarded as statistically reliable, which is acknowledged by the agency's officials themselves. From the early 1950s onward the United Nations General Assembly repeatedly instructed them to supply reliable data,[13] but this was not done. The names of deceased refugees from 1950 onward were only partly deleted from the lists of those eligible for allocations of food provisions and other forms of support (especially housing) that the agency provided. Furthermore, thorough and ongoing updating of death records, a prerequisite of reliable data, was not instituted. Clearly, the population involved, and the UNRWA bureaucracy itself, had an interest in preserving the inflated lists in order to gain extra food rations for households and larger allocations for services (education, health, housing, etc.) in the camps. Thus, according

Table 1.8

Syria: registered Palestinian refugees, 1960-87 (selected years)

	Males	Females	Total
1960	65,031	61,631	126,662
1965	78,239	73,945	152,184
1970	92,573	87,763	180,336
1975	104,398	99,979	204,376
1980	121,735	116,483	238,218
1985	137,803	131,973	269,776
1987	144,395	138,278	282,673

Source: J'AS, *MΓA 1985*, p. 79, table 2/21;*1986*, p.80, table 2/22; *1988*, p. 67, table 2/17.

to UNRWA data the death rates in the camps were around 2.5 per thousand[14] — an unlikely figure. The skewed nature of the UNRWA data — high regarding total population of the camps and low regarding death rates — precludes utilizing them as a basis for evaluating rates of natural increase.

Given the sparsity of data, it is common practice to regard the natural increase rates of the total population in each country that has a large Palestinian community as applying to the Palestinian population as well. This approach has several flaws. First, the data on natural increase rates in several of the relevant Arab states are unreliable. For example, calculations of the natural increase rates in Lebanon are based on a population census of 1932; the data published by Jordan and Syria are flawed by underregistration of number of deaths;[15] and Saudi Arabia has no published accurate figure for its total population for the period under study.[16]

Even if the data on natural increase rates in these countries were reliable, it would still be impossible to extrapolate demographic figures for the Palestinian communities, as there is no empirical or theoretical basis for assuming that the natural increase rates among the Palestinians are identical to those of the population as a whole. The few cases where a comparison between the overall natural increase rate and the specific rate of the Palestinian population can be made show that this assumption is untenable. For example, according to data published by the Jordanian government, the average natural increase for the entire population of Jordan, including the West Bank in 1965–70, was about 33 per thousand.[17] But separate data for the West Bank for 1968–70 show that natural increase rates there were far lower — 23 per thousand (see table 1.7), a discrepancy so great that it cannot be attributed to incidental influences or short-term factors.

Lastly, even if exact data on births and deaths in the Palestinian communities dispersed throughout the Arab countries were available, this still would not be adequate for calculating the size of these populations and their natural increase rates because of considerable migratory movement in some of these communities over long periods, and the absence of reliable data on Palestinian migratory movement in the period under consideration. Hence, the size of the Palestinian communities outside Israel, the West Bank and Gaza can only be estimated. For this purpose the demographic data on the Muslim population in Israel and the Palestinian population in the West Bank and the Gaza Strip may be useful in determining the upper limits of the natural increase rates. It is reasonable to assume that the total Palestinian population did not increase at the same rate as the Muslim population in Israel. The gap we have noted between the Muslims in Israel on the one hand, and the Palestinians of the West Bank and the Gaza Strip on the other, provides sufficient grounds for this assumption. In other words, we can assume that the total Palestinian population did not increase at an average annual rate of 42 per thousand during 1949-87 (the rate for the Muslims in Israel), but at a lower rate. How much lower? The partial figures available support the conclusion that the average annual increase rate was closer to the natural increase rates in the West Bank and the Gaza Strip during the 1970s and 1980s, that is, between 31 and 35 per thousand. The aggregate figure for the total population, 4.6 million at the end of 1987, falls within these limits.

EXTERNAL MIGRATION

The second major demographic process that characterized the Palestinian population, or more precisely a significant part of it, from 1949 onward was external migration. This trend, whose rate varied during this period, was a result of the high concentration of refugees in the West Bank and the Gaza Strip at the end of the 1948 war and the limited economic potential and investment in those areas during the period under discussion. Added to this was the growing demand for workers in the Arab oil economies of the Persian Gulf and within Jordan itself (East Bank).

The largest migratory movement consisted of both refugees and permanent residents from the West Bank (followed by the Gaza Strip) moving to the East Bank. From there some of the migrants continued on to the Persian Gulf states, chiefly Kuwait and Saudi Arabia. In some cases migrants moved directly from the West Bank or the Gaza Strip to one of the Gulf oil states. The principal push force responsible for this migration was economic hardship in the West Bank and Gaza Strip, characterized by high unemployment (open and hidden) and low per capita income. At the same time, powerful pull forces were at work: economic development on the East Bank leading to job opportunities, and plentiful employment opportunities offering high incomes in the oil states beginning in the 1950s and peaking in the 1970s. Significantly, Jordan did not hinder Palestinians wishing to enter the East Bank throughout this period, whether for employment and permanent residence or as a way station in migration further east to the Persian Gulf.

In fact, the Jordanian government invested considerable resources in facilitating the absorption of the Palestinian workers in the East Bank, and also promoted the interests of Palestinians in the oil states who resided there as holders of Jordanian passports.[18] In this context, the wave of eastward migration from the West Bank and Gaza Strip during and following the June war of 1967 (according to CBS estimates, about 173,000 people left the West Bank in June–August 1967) should be viewed primarily as a reaction to a political upheaval rather than as a response to economic forces.[19]

In assessing the total number of Palestinians who left the West Bank and Gaza Strip during the forty years under discussion, figures of about 2.0 million in the West Bank and about 850,000 in the Gaza Strip might have been estimated for the end of 1987 had the balance of migration from both areas been zero. The actual figures, however, were 860,000 and 594,000, respectively, revealing a negative migration balance of about 1.14 million in the West Bank and about 250,000 in the Gaza Strip. These figures, which total 1.39 million, are equal to the aggregate increase of the two largest concentrations of Palestinians outside the boundaries of western Palestine (Israel, the West Bank and Gaza Strip) during the period under study: in Jordan (East Bank) and in the Arab oil states in the Gulf. The number of Palestinians in Jordan increased from approximately 70,000 in 1949 to about 1.2 million in 1987, and in the Arab oil states from several hundred to about 500,000 in the same period. Subtracting the 1948 refugee population and its progeny, as well as migrants from Lebanon and Syria in Jordan, the result is about 1.4 million, or the number of migrants and their progeny from the West Bank and Gaza Strip.

The negative migration balance from the West Bank accounts for the major shift in foci of concentration of the Palestinian population after 1949. In that year, 80 percent of the total Palestinian population (1.06 million out of 1.32 million people) lived within the boundaries of western Palestine. By 1987, the proportion of the population living there had dropped to about 47 percent (2.14 million out of 4.60 million), while the eastward migratory movement had created two new (or nearly new) major concentrations of the Palestinian population, in Jordan and in the Persian Gulf region. By 1987 the number of Palestinians in these two regions exceeded that in the two other largest concentrations (outside Israel), namely, the West Bank and Gaza Strip.

The Palestinians in Israel had a small positive migration balance,

24

which together with high natural increase rates led to a sharp rise in their proportion within the entire Palestinian population of western Palestine.[20] In 1949 the Arabs in Israel accounted for 14 percent of this population; by 1987 this proportion (not including East Jerusalem) had risen to 34 percent. Their proportion in the total Palestinian population increased from 11 to about 16 percent.

An analysis of the existing data and estimates shows that at the end of 1987, about four decades after the 1948 war, the Palestinians were dispersed in six main political and economic units as follows:

(1)   The West Bank and the Gaza Strip: 1.42 million (see table 1.6). It is reasonable to assume that this figure is higher — probably by at least 200,000 — but there is no way of determining the extent of the deviation with certainty.

(2)   Jordan: about 1.2 million. This figure is based on estimates of natural increase rates, migration balance, and analysis of data on the size of Palestinian communities in other countries. This estimate does not include Palestinians carrying Jordanian passports who lived outside Jordan for one year or more.

(3)   Israel (including East Jerusalem): 718,000 (see table 1.5). This is the only figure that is based on a relatively recent population census (1982) and current annual updating.

(4)   Kuwait: about 300,000. This figure is based on Kuwaiti population census reports from the 1970s which include data on the number of Jordanian nationals in Kuwait (see table 1.9). It is generally accepted that about 95 percent of all Jordanian passport-holders in Kuwait were Palestinian.[21] However, census reports from the 1980s do not indicate the specific number of

Table 1.9

Kuwait: Jordanian nationals,[a] 1965, 1970 and 1975[b]

	Males	Females	Total
1965	49,744	27,968	77,712
1970	79,934	67,762	147,696
1975	107,770	96,408	204,178

Notes:
a   Including Palestinians holding Jordanian passports.
b   Census figures.
Source: DK, MIS 1980, p. 28, table 24.

Jordanian nationals within the total population of Arab citizens (bearers of passports from Arab states) resident in Kuwait.[22] Hence, estimates of the number of Palestinians in Kuwait are based on a combination of census data; unofficial estimates of Palestinian migration to Kuwait in the 1980s; estimates of the proportion of Palestinians within the total population of Jordanian nationals in Kuwait; estimates of the natural increase rate among the Palestinians there; and the number of Palestinians illegally residing in Kuwait. The figure of 300,000 does not include Palestinians who became naturalized Kuwaiti citizens between 1949 and 1987 (apparently some 40,000–50,000).

(5) & (6) Lebanon: about 270,000, and Syria: about 240,000. These estimates are based on partial data and gross evaluations. The lack of solid data has given rise to a wide range of estimates. For example, the statistical yearbook published by the PLO gave the size of the Palestinian population in Lebanon in 1981 as 492,000 (see table 1.10).

Table 1.10

The Palestinians: population estimates by place of residence 1980-84, according to PLO publications

(in thousands)

	1980	1981	1982	1983	1984	1985
Israel	531	551	551	575	581	603
West Bank	818	833	833	872	893	919
Gaza Strip	477	451	452	476	494	510
Jordan	1,161	1,148	1,148	1,190	1,248	1,298
Lebanon	347	358	492	492	492	492
Syria	216	223	223	230	237	247
Kuwait	279	300	295	308	322	337
Saudi Arabia						
UAE, Qatar	184	198	198	212	225	239
Other Arab states	140	141	130	133	134	138
USA	102	105	105	108	111	114
Other states	136	140	140	144	148	152
Total	4,390	4,447	4,566	4,739	4,885	5,046

Sources: PLO, *MIF 1980*, no. 2, p. 28; *1981*, no. 3, p. 30; *1982*, no. 4, p. 32, *1983*, no. 5, p. 36; *1984-1985*, no. 6, p. 42.

26

Based on the above estimates, of the countries with large Palestinian communities in 1987 (excluding the West Bank and Gaza Strip) only in Jordan did the Palestinians constitute 50 percent or more of the total population in the country (some estimates place the figure at 55-60 percent).[23] Nevertheless, their proportion in three other states was substantial: in Israel, about 18 percent; in Kuwait, about 15 percent; and in Lebanon, about 10 percent.

The statistical yearbooks published by the PLO Office of Statistics (al-Majmu'a al-ihsa'iyya al-filastiniyya) contain estimates and evaluations of the major concentrations of the Palestinian population from 1980 onward (see table 1.10), but these figures seem inflated. For example, the total number of Palestinians for 1981 is given as 4.57 million. Even assuming relatively low natural increase rates of 25 per thousand for the entire Palestinian population thereafter, during 1982-87, a figure of 5.3 million at the end of 1987 would be obtained. Even PLO leaders did not posit a Palestinian population of 5.3 million in 1987, although they put the size of the Palestinian diaspora at 3.5 million in April 1989.[24] The upward deviation is especially marked for the estimated size of the Palestinian populations in Lebanon, Saudi Arabia and the Gulf emirates.

URBANIZATION

The process of urbanization, a dynamic social development among the Palestinians during the Mandate period, underwent far-reaching changes in the forty years following the end of the 1948 war. Two main trends can be identified: de-urbanization for the Arabs in Israel and East Jerusalem, and increased urbanization for the rest of the Palestinian communities, including the West Bank.

The Arab community in Israel did not undergo a process of urbanization during the period under review. The combined population of the three main Arab urban centers in Israel — Nazareth, Umm al-Fahm and Shafa'amr — increased from 28,300 in 1950 to 91,100 in 1987, or 325 percent,[25] while Israel's total Arab population (including Druze) increased by about 407 percent during the same period. A somewhat different perspective gives a similar picture: in 1987, Israel's 11 largest Arab settlements (with populations of at least 10,000) accounted for 31 percent of the total Arab population (including Druze), while in 1955 these settlements had accounted for about 34 percent (see table 1.11). During the period of military government in the Arab localities in Israel (1949–66), Arabs were not permitted to move to the "mixed" Arab-Jewish cities (Jerusalem, Haifa, Tel Aviv-Jaffa, Acre, Lod and Ramla) except in special circumstances. After 1966, social factors kept the rates of migration to the cities low: the preference for living in an all-Arab community on the one hand, and feelings of alienation from the Jewish population on the other, inhibited movement even to the mixed cities, let alone to the all-Jewish ones. Economic factors were also involved: urban housing costs were higher than rural. In addition, the development of transport and communications networks narrowed the advantages which city living offered in terms of accessibility to workplaces.[26] These factors explain the lack of large-scale migratory movement to the towns where rural Arabs were employed, despite pressure on

Table 1.11

Israel: Arab population in localities with over 10,000 inhabitants in 1955 and 1987[a]

(end of year)

	1955	1987	Change in percent
Umm al-Fahm	6,100	23,100	279
Baqa al-Gharbiyya	3,800	13,200	247
Tayba[b]	6,100	19,500	220
Tira	4,500	12,700	182
Tamra	4,300	14,900	247
Mghar	3,400	12,100	256
Nazareth	23,000	49,400	115
Sakhnin	4,300	14,800	244
Arraba[b]	2,900	11,200	286
Rahat		16,800	
Shafa'amr	5,400	19,400	259
Haifa[c]	8,700	19,800	128
Tel Aviv-Jaffa[c]	5,700	10,800	89

Notes:
a Excluding East Jerusalem.
b Including non-Arab Christian inhabitants.
c Including Baha'i and non-Arab Christian inhabitants.
Sources: CBS, *ASI 1988*, pp. 60–61, table 2/15.

28

the Arab villages' economic resources. This pressure resulted not in migration, but in a growing vocational shift away from traditional agriculture to services and industry, and more marginally to modern agriculture, in the Jewish sector. By 1987, 52 percent of Arab workers were employed outside their places of residence.[27]

Nevertheless, some migratory movement from villages in northern Israel toward Haifa began in the 1980s, leading to an increase in the city's Arab population both in absolute terms and in relation to the size of the Jewish population. This migratory movement, however, did not extend to the all-Arab cities because of an absence of pull forces. The Arab cities, such as Nazareth and Shafa'amr, had limited available land for construction, undeveloped urban infrastructures, and most importantly, insufficient job opportunities.

In East Jerusalem, which had experienced a process of de-urbanization throughout the period of Jordanian rule, the population grew, after 1967, at a rate that only slightly exceeded the natural increase rate of its Arab residents, so that total increase for the entire 1946–87 period — from 87,000 to 137,000, or about 57 percent[28] — was lower than the rate that would have been obtained through the natural increase rate of the city's Arab inhabitants.

While several towns in the West Bank experienced a similar process of de-urbanization, with slow population increase characterizing Hebron and Qalqiliya during Jordanian rule, and Nablus, al-Bira, Bayt Jala, Qabatiya and Bayt Sahur under Israeli rule, the rate of population growth in the majority of the West Bank towns exceeded the natural increase rates of the population. Moreover, the proportion of the urban population in the West Bank increased from about 25 percent in 1947 to about 50 percent in 1987 (see table 1.12). Most of this rise occurred in the 1980s and was a result of movement by the refugees from the camps to the cities. In several cases refugee camps were annexed to municipal areas of jurisdiction.[29] In sum, Palestinian society in the West Bank underwent a process of urbanization, a change with significant social, economic and political implications.

Refugee camps established in 1948–49 in the countries of the Arab diaspora were set up near or within towns, or were integrated into existing urban frameworks. Thus, the majority of the Palestinian population in the Persian Gulf states, Jordan, Syria and Lebanon found employment in cities. Only a small minority of Palestinians settled in villages, mainly in Jordan.

Table 1.12
*West Bank: Palestinian population in localities with over 10,000
inhabitants in 1967 and 1987*
(end of year)

	1967	1987	Change in percent
Nablus	61,053	106,944	75
Hebron	38,309	79,087	106
Bethlehem	16,313	34,180	110
Tul Karm	15,275	30,151	97
Jenin	13,365	26,318	97
Ramallah	12,134	24,772	104
al-Bira	13,037	22,540	73
Yatta	7,281	20,755	185
Qalqiliya	8,926	18,972	113
Dura	4,954	13,420	171
Jericho	5,312	12,528	136
Dhahiriya	4,875	11,519	136
Bayt Jala	6,041	10,976	82
Qabatiya	6,005	10,823	80
Tubas	5,262	10,635	102
Bayt Sahur	5,380	10,077	87

Source: *The West Bank and Gaza Atlas*, pp. 125–37, appendix 1.

Although no country has published data on the distribution of its Palestinian population by location or employment, partial and indirect data indicate that by 1987 the great majority (up to 80 percent) of all Palestinians in the Arab diaspora lived in cities or nearby camps.[30] From this standpoint, the eastward migration entailed an additional basic demographic change — a high rate of urbanization. This development was attributable primarily to economic conditions in the migrants' destinations. The search for work in the various countries of destination was concentrated in services and industry, as agriculture played a fairly marginal role in these economies and the potential for agricultural development was limited. Thus, the great majority of the migrants were absorbed into urban centers.[31]

CONCLUSION

The rapid growth of the Palestinian population in the West Bank and the Gaza Strip and in Israel on the one hand, and the slower growth of the Jewish population in Israel during most of the 1980s on the other, raised the issue of demographic balance between Jews and Arabs in Eretz Israel/Palestine. The debates that ensued among the Jewish public as well as among the Palestinian leadership on the political implications of this demographic development took their cues both from trends during the 1970s and 1980s and from forecasts of the CBS which gave projections of the size of the Palestinian population in Israel and the territories for the 1990s and the start of the twenty-first century. A CBS forecast published in 1987 predicted that the proportion of the Arab population in Israel would rise to 21.5 percent in the year 2000 and that the Palestinians would constitute 50 percent of the total population in Israel and the occupied territories by 2015.[32] This forecast was based on several assumptions, the most important being little change in the birth and mortality rates of the Palestinian and Jewish populations, along with the continuation of 1985–87 trends regarding population movement of both Jews and Palestinians (small positive and negative migration balances).

The demographic issue elicited diametrically opposed conclusions within the Israeli public. On the one hand, current demographic developments strengthened the conviction of those who believed that the territories had to be abandoned by Israel wholly or in part, and that local self-government in one from or another had to be instituted, principally in the main Palestinian population centers in the Gaza Strip and the West Bank.[33] On the other hand, these same developments, along with the CBS forecasts, reinforced the position of those who favored population "transfer" — enforced or "voluntary" — and the "Jordan-is-Palestine" view.[34]

The PLO also focused increasingly on the implications of demographic developments in the territories and in Israel during 1980s, its reactions largely a mirror image of attitudes in Israel. PLO leaders, especially in the Fath, regarded the changing proportions of the Jewish and Arab populations not only as a welcome development but also as an important tool in the Palestinian struggle against Israel. As such, demography was an effective weapon even in the short term, in that it threatened Israel and fomented serious disagreement within it. According to this view, the threat of Palestinian demographic growth was likely to bring about an Israeli recognition that there was no escape from the establishment of a Palestinian state in the West Bank and Gaza. In the long term, the Palestinian demographic advantage would see Israel reduced to the point where it would disappear as a Zionist state.[35] When Arafat voiced this approach in a statement in November 1987, it quickly became a Palestinian slogan in the territories: "The Palestinian woman, who bears yet another Palestinian every ten months... is a biological bomb that threatens to blow up Israel from within."[36]

Yet, in the Palestinian camp too there was debate over the political implications of demographic development in the occupied territories. Fears mounted in the PLO that the graver the demographic menace to Israel, the greater the threat of mass deportation of Palestinians from the territories by Israel, especially when in the late 1980s the idea of "transfer" was discussed openly in Israel. The PLO feared that inflated use of the demographic argument to influence political positions in Israel vis-à-vis the national goals of the Palestinians might become a double-edged sword. Moreover, the Democratic Front for the Liberation of Palestine, the Popular Front for the Liberation of Palestine and, to some extent, Fath claimed that overdependence on the demographic advantage as a means of bringing about change in the Palestinian situation was dangerous as it could lead to inaction among Palestinians generally and the population in the territories in particular.[37] Hence, after several years of intense promotion of the promise inherent in demographic development, PLO leaders adopted a more restrained position on this issue.

NOTES

1. UN Conciliation Commission for Palestine, *Final Report of the U.N. Economic Survey Mission for the Middle East*, 28 December 1949, U.N. Doc. A/AC.25/6 (hereafter: *Survey Mission Report 1949*). The data presented in table 2.1 are based on estimates of the Survey Mission. Several figures have been altered in the light of studies published in the 1970s and 1980s. See A. S. al-Dajani et al., *al-Filastiniyyun fi'l-watan al-'arabi*, Cairo: 1978, p. 128.
2. According to the *Survey Mission Report 1949*, 7,000 Palestinians left for Egypt and 4,000 for Iraq.
3. The population of Transjordan (the East Bank) was estimated at the end of 1947 at 375,000. At the end of 1949 it was estimated at about 400,000, and with the addition of the refugees at about 470,000. See IBRD, *The Economic Development of Jordan*, Baltimore: Johns Hopkins Press, 1957, p. 49, table 1 (hereafter: IBRD, *Jordan*).

4. See especially the periodicals *Statistical Quarterly of the Occupied Areas* (1973-81) and *JSGAS* (1982-90), as well as the chapter covering the West Bank and Gaza Strip in *SAI.*

5. The statistical yearbooks published by the PLO contain data on the Palestinian population in Israel, the West Bank and the Gaza Strip, taken from current volumes of CBS, *SAI.* See Munazamat al-tahrir al-filastiniyya, al-Maktab al-markazi li'l-ihsa'a, *al-Majmu'a al-ihsa'iyya al-filastiniyya*, 1980-1985, nos. 2-6, Damascus, 1980-1986 (hereafter: PLO, *MIF*).

6. See Meron Benvenisti et al., "Demography (Palestinian)" in *The West Bank Handbook*, Jerusalem: 1986, p. 51 (hereafter: *The West Bank Handbook*); Meron Benvenisti and Shlomo Khayat, *The West Bank and Gaza Atlas*, Jerusalem: The West Bank Data Base Project, 1988, pp. 27-30 (hereafter: *The West Bank and Gaza Atlas*).

7. Since the 1960s (especially after the 1967 June war) a large number of estimates on the size and geographical distribution of the Palestinian population have been published. Most of these estimates are not based on the study of demographic trends among the Palestinians, and some of them suffer from over- or underestimation. See, for example, Janet L. Abu-Lughod, "The Demographic Transformation of Palestine," in Ibrahim A. Abu-Lughod (ed.), *The Transformation of Palestine*, Evanston: Northwestern University Press, 1971, p. 163; Nabil Shaath, "High-Level Palestinian Manpower," *JPS* 1/2 (1972): 81; J.F. Jraissaty, "La dispersion palestinienne," *Khamsin* 2 (1975): 27, table 1; Moshe Efrat, *ha-Plitim ha-palestina'im. Mehqar kalkali we-hevrati, 1949-1974*, Tel Aviv: David Horowitz Institute, 1976, appendices. George Kossaifi, "Demographic Characteristics of the Arab Palestinian People," in Khalil Nakhleh and Elia Zureik (eds.), *The Sociology of the Palestinians*, London: Croom Helm, 1980, pp. 20 and 31, tables 1.3 and 1.4; Janet L. Abu-Lughod, *Demographic Characteristics of the Palestinian Population: Relevance for Planning Palestine Open University*, Paris: UNESCO, 1980, pp. 11-13, table 1; Nabil Badran, "Palestinian Migration Trends and Socio-Economic Consequences," UN, Economic Commission for Western Asia, Conference on International Migration in the Arab World, Beirut, May 1981, pp. 9-10, table 1; Iris Agmon, *ha-Pzura ha-palestinit ba-'olam, 1948-1982: hebetim demografiyyim, hevratiyyim we-kalkaliyyim* (mimeograph), Tel Aviv: The Shiloah Institute, 1983, pp. 12-20 (hereafter: Agmon); Allen B. Hill, "The Palestinian Population of the Middle East," *Population and Development Review* 9/2 (1983): 295, table 1; Z. Sa'id et al., *al-Waqi al-filastini. al-Madi wa'l-hadir wa'l-mustaqbal*, Cairo, 1986, p. 56, table 1; p. 62, table 2; Lisa Hajjar, "The Palestinian Journey, 1952-1987," *MERIP Middle East Report* 17/3 (1987): p. 10. See also table 1.10 below, which contains the estimates for the years 1980-84 given in PLO, *MIF*, nos. 2-6.

8. See CBS, *SAI 1968*, p. 55, table 3/3; *1988*, p. 33, table 2/2. Cf. Dov Friedlander and Calvin Goldscheider, "Israel's Population: The Challenge of Pluralism," *Population Bulletin* 39/2 (1984): 22, table 4 (hereafter: Friedlander and Goldscheider).

9. According to CBS, *SAI 1954*, p. 15, table 12; *1960*, p. 33, table 2; *1988*, p. 94, table 3/1. For a discussion of the fertility rates of Muslim women in Israel see Friedlander and Goldscheider, pp. 26-28.

10. See also CBS, *JSGAS*, vol. 22 (1993).

11. J'AS, al-Maktab al-markazi li'l-ihsa'a, *al-Majmu'a al-ihsa'iyya li-'amm 1988*, no. 41, Damascus, 1988 (hereafter: J'AS, *MI'A*).

12. *Annual Report of the Director of the United Nations Relief and Works Agency for Palestine Refugees in the Near East*, General Assembly Official Records, Supplement no. 13, 1954/5 (hereafter: *UNRWA Report*).

13. An unequivocal demand for updating the lists of those eligible for food rations was put before UNRWA in June 1958 by the Secretary-General Dag Hammerskold in a report he submitted to the 14th session of the General Assembly. See *Proposals for the Continuation of United Nations Assistance to Palestin Refugees Submitted by the Secretary-General to the 14th Session of the General Assembly*, 15 June 1958, UN Doc. A/4121.

14. According to *UNRWA Reports* for the years 1969-79.
15. U. Schmelz, "ha-Hitpathut ha-demografit shel ha-medinot ha-'arviyot be-ezorenu", *Hamizrah Hehadash* 22 (1972): 449; 23 (1973): 30-31.
16. Eliane Domschke and Doreen S. Goyer, *The Handbook of National Population Censuses, Africa and Asia*, New York: Greenwood Press, 1986, pp. 807-8.
17. UN, *Demographic Yearbook 1970*, New York: United Nations, 1970, p. 121, table 3 (hereafter: *Demographic Yearbook*).
18. Michael P. Mazur, *Economic Growth and Development in Jordan*, Boulder: Westview Press, 1979, p. 32 (hereafter: Mazur).
19. Yaacov Lifshitz, *ha-Hitpathut ha-kalkalit ba-shtahim ha-muhzaqim, 1967-1969*, Tel Aviv: Ma'arakhot, 1970, pp. 31-32. Cf. HKJ, *The Tragedy of Arab Refugees, Facts and Figures*, Amman, 1968; Mazur, pp. 81, 87; F.A. Gharaibeh, *The Economies of the West Bank and the Gaza Strip*, Boulder and London: Westview Press, 1985, p. 30.
20. The balance of migration of the Arabs of Israel (including Druzes and 'others') in the period 1948-87 amounted to 9,900 people. Most of the increment (4,800 people) was in 1972-82. See CBS, *SAI 1988*, p. 32, table 2/2.
21. DK, *MIS*, vol. 23, 1986, p. 27, table 13.
22. The authors of PLO, *MIF* (p. 237) estimate that the proportion of Palestinians in the "Jordanian" population in Kuwait reached (until 1990) 95 percent. See also B. al-Hasan, *al-Filastiniyyun fi'l kuwayt*, Beirut, 1974, p. 11, note.
23. *al-Majalla* (London), 6 January 1989.
24. *al-Watan al-'Arabi*, 21 April 1989.
25. CBS, *SAI 1988*, pp. 60-61, table 2/15.
26. The figure for 1946 relates to the total Muslim and Christian inhabitants living in the area of jurisdiction of the Jerusalem municipality in 1967. See U. Schmeltz, "ha-Demografya shel ha-muslemim we-ha-notzrim be-yerushalayyim," *Hamizrah Hehadash* 28 (1979): 43, table 3. The figure for 1987 also includes the Arab population (Muslim and Christian) residing in the western part of the city. See CBS, *SAI 1988*, p. 60, table 2/15.
27. See, e.g., Mazur, pp. 28-29; Laurie A. Brand, *Palestinians in the Arab World*, New York: Columbia University Press, 1988, p. 117 (hereafter: Brand).
28. U. Schmeltz, "ha-Tifroset ha-merhavit shel ha-'aravim we-ha-druzim be-yisrael u-meafyenei yeshuveihem," *Hamizrah Hehadash* 29 (1980): 100-1.
29. CBS, *SAI 1988*, p. 358, table 12/19.
30. Emanuel Marx, "Palestinian Refugee Camps in the West Bank and the Gaza Strip," *MES* 28/2 (1992): 285-86.
31. Agmon, pp. 37-39; Brand, pp. 116-17.
32. CBS, *Special Report*, no. 802 (1987).
33. Yehoshafat Harkabi, *Hahlatot goraliyot*, Tel Aviv: Am Oved, 1986, pp. 60-69.
34. "Transfer: be'ad ve-neged," *Ha-umma* 88 (1987): 11-19.
35. Matti Steinberg, "ha-Gorem ha-demographi ba-sikhsush 'im Israel be-'eyney Ashaf," *Medina, Mimshal ve-Yahasim Beynleumiyyim* 31 (1989): 38 (hereafter: Steinberg).
36. *al-Akhbar* (Cairo), 3 July 1987.
37. Steinberg, pp. 31, 36.

2

Background to Migration:
The Case of Nablus, 1949-56

NABLUS AFTER THE ANNEXATION

A major trade center in northern Palestine since Ottoman times, Nablus in 1948 had a population of ca. 45,000. Even before the formal annexation of the West Bank by the Hashemite Kingdom of Jordan, on 30 April 1950, the town's leadership had begun exerting pressure on the Jordanian government to assume responsibility for the economic functions that earlier had been fulfilled by the Mandatory administration. With the worsening of the economic crisis that hit Nablus in the early 1950s, various sectors began clamoring for government action to help the city's economy adapt to the changing circumstances thrown up by the war and the subsequent influx of tens of thousands of refugees.

First were the large landowners, who demanded government assistance for development of the farms they owned in the areas to the east of the city and in the Jordan Valley (Ghur Nablus, Ghur al-Far'a, Ghur al-Badan and Ghur al-Jiftlik). During the summer of 1949 and the winter of 1950 several assemblies took place in the city at the initiative of this group requesting the government to complete the Jordan Valley irrigation scheme that the Mandatory government had begun, so as to permit the enlargement of the irrigated and cultivated land there by at least 20,000 dunams (5,000 acres). Wahid al-Masri, one of the largest landowners in the Ghur and the driving spirit behind this effort, also demanded the improvement of the drainage system, the implementation of programs for soil improvement

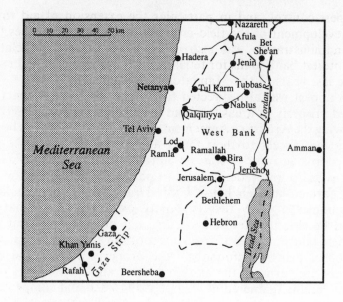

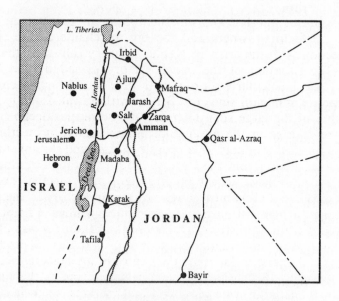

Illustration 2.1
Jordan: West Bank, East Bank, 1949

and pest control, and in particular the extension of aid toward the development of the field-crop and dairy-farm branches.[1] The new administration was also called upon to arrange relatively low-interest bank loans for fellahin, such as those that had existed in the last years of the Mandatory government.[2]

An appeal was also directed to Amman by city residents who owned property in areas that had become part of Israeli territory following the Armistice Agreement. When property owners became aware that access to their fields and orchards — for the most part, citrus groves — was no longer possible, they asked the authorities to intercede in order to obtain special access for West Bank farmers to their lands within Israeli boundaries. As late as the summer of 1949 these property owners believed that they would be able to harvest and carry out other agricultural work on their land in Israel if the king took up this issue.[3] But when this belief proved unfounded, "the property owners, the citrus growers, the farmers, the bank managers and the notables of the city of Nablus" gathered in August 1949 to demand compensation "for those whose lands have been plundered and attached to the Jewish territory."[4]

Pressure of another kind on the Jordanian government came from the factory owners and the big merchants of the city in connection with the crisis in Nablus industry following the 1948 war. The situation of the match factory owned by the Masri family was particularly serious, with production having come to a complete standstill since the British withdrawal. Equally grave was that of the large soap factories, whose output declined by a high percentage in the absence of administrative protection for local industrial products. Against this background the government was called upon, from the start of 1950, to prohibit competitive imports or at least to set up a system of protective excises.[5] Moreover, 'Arif al-Nabulsi, owner of a soap factory in the town, speaking for many of his colleagues in the chamber of commerce, insisted that the Ministry of Commerce and Industry was obliged to take steps to encourage the export of local industrial products.[6] A similar demand to facilitate the export of agricultural products was voiced by the big landowners in Nablus and at their urging also by the fellahin, who requested that markets for their surplus produce be found.[7]

An even livelier struggle was conducted by the city merchants against the policy of import quotas that the finance and commerce ministries pursued owing to the limited foreign currency reserves available to the Jordanian economy. In the first years following annexation it became customary for no more than a third of all import licenses to be granted to West Bank importers.[8] This overt preference for East Bank merchants, as well as delays in issuing licenses and other obstacles placed in the path of the West Bank importers, aroused great resentment in Nablus. On 18 February 1950 representatives of all the West Bank chambers of commerce convened in the city for a meeting to which Minister of Trade Khalusi al-Khayri was also invited.[9] The nature of the complaint directed against the minister on that occasion was reiterated about two months later in a joint letter of protest sent to Amman by all the chambers of commerce on the West Bank, a précis of which was published in *al-Difa'*:

> The question of imports is still the major problem of the West Bank. There are distinctions and preferences between the importers of the East and those of the West Bank. The West Bank merchants worked hard and spent much time in order to obtain a share of the [licenses to] import at the end of 1949. They believed that this would provide an opportunity to improve the situation in the future, but they were mistaken. Their case did not get a fair hearing. The situation at present is that the importers are divided into two groups: [those of] the East Bank and [those of] the West Bank. The first group has won a favorable attitude and preference on the part of the authorities. The second has not... The importers and the merchants on the West Bank are bitter about the lack of equality between the two banks in economic matters.[10]

Another discontented group in the city who exerted pressure on the government to solve their problem were the unemployed. Refugees formed the major, although not the sole, component of the unemployed in Nablus. They organized themselves with the aim of pressuring the government and UNRWA to increase work opportunities, primarily by reactivating the Arab-Palestinian Workers' Union (*Jam'iyat al-'ummal al-'arabiyya al-filastiniyya*), whose center was established in Nablus in 1949. Leading the struggle of the unemployed refugees for integration into the city's economy, the union, in the summer of 1949, began to register all job-seekers in Nablus and, together with the refugee committees in the city, demanded piecework in order to employ them.[11] A convention of representatives of all the union branches on the West Bank, organized by the center in Nablus in October 1950, was attended by 20 delegates who called on the government to fight unemployment by creating piecework in construction and industry.[12] In addition, both refugees and local residents submitted increasingly angry appeals, letters of protest and petitions to government officials in the city and to the authorities in Amman demanding work.[13]

In 1951 and 1952 the Jordanian Workers Union (*Jam'iyat al-'ummal al-'urduniyya*) arranged various assemblies to draw the government's attention to the hardships suffered by the unemployed.[14] During this period unemployment struck many veteran Nablus residents as well, prompting the city council to join in the chorus of voices demanding government initiatives on the issue.[15] Articles describing the severity of the problem appeared in the dailies *Filastin* and *al-Jihad*.[16] By the latter half of 1952, migration from the city eastward to the oil-producing countries had become a phenomenon that affected all aspects of the city's economy. Hafiz al-Hamadallah, a Nablus delegate in the Jordanian parliament, called on the prime minister to set up "employment enterprises" in the city and its environs without delay.[17]

Moreover, in light of the high levels of unemployment and inflation that burdened the Jordanian economy during 1949-52, leading public figures in Nablus demanded that the government institute price controls for basic consumer goods that would adjust the supply of goods and services on both banks, as well as make welfare payments to the needy.[18]

THE GOVERNMENT'S RESPONSE

The response of the Jordanian government to these expectations and demands during the five years following the 1948 war was limited, and the sum total of its operations in the economic sphere was meager. The only activities of any importance were those undertaken by the Ministry of Agriculture, the district authority, and the other government offices responsible for promoting economic activity in the villages surrounding the city. Instruction and assistance was provided to the fellahin in combatting soil erosion and pests, supplying seed and mechanized equipment, prospecting for water sources, and piping water to villages whose wells had dried up.[19] Although providing these services had already been a matter of routine, the government did not always succeed in fulfilling all requirements at the right time or place.[20] The ministry also began to seek ways of developing the irrigation system in the Jordan Valley and approved a long-term loan of JD 100,000 to Ghur landowners for this purpose in August 1952.[21]

In an attempt to satisfy the fellahin's demand to renew loan arrangements, the government established the Agricultural Bank *(al-Bank al-zira'i)*, which began to make loans of several dozen dinars each.[22] Since such sums were inadequate for development needs, the government encouraged local fellahin to invest in the development of their farms from their own resources.[23] Most of the programs designed for the agricultural development of rural areas, however, were not implemented. A plan to set up a number of model villages "along the lines of the Jewish settlements" was the subject of lengthy discussions but was not realized.[24] The only plans to be carried out were for the afforestation of areas near the city, tobacco and cotton cultivation in the Jordan Valley, and expansion of olive groves.[25]

The pressure by the Nablus factory owners to protect local manufactured goods and to aid exports elicited limited response. Although the import of competing products such as soap and matches was barred in 1952, this ban lasted only a few months.[26] The government did obtain the consent of the Egyptian government in 1950 to grant preferred status to the import of soaps and oils produced on the West Bank, reducing customs tariffs.[27] Direct investment in the development of Nablus industry was also considered by the Jordanian government. In December 1953 the Ministry of Economy expressed interest in acquiring shares worth JD 30,000 for the establishment of an oil factory in the city on condition that a further JD 70,000, which was required for the construction of the plant, be procured by the private sector.[28] However, several years were to pass before the government acted on this project.

The most serious of the economic problems that plagued the city — unemployment — was left to UNRWA and the city council to contend with. The government public works department provided only a limited amount of piecework in Nablus.[29] While an UNRWA proposal to settle refugees on state-owned agricultural land elicited government agreement to place such lands at the disposal of the agency, the government made it clear that UNRWA would be obliged to carry out all necessary development work.[30] Moreover, once the Nablus city council decided to use the unemployed work force in the city to develop its municipal services, government assistance became minimal.

In April 1950 the council resolved to implement a large-scale development plan at an investment of JD 60,000, which was enlarged within a few months to an estimated expenditure of JD 100,000.[31] The extended plan was submitted for approval to the council of ministers, together with a request that the government guarantee a loan for this amount, which the Ottoman Bank had agreed to grant. Only in March 1952, however, about two years after the initial approach by the municipality, did the council of ministers agree to guarantee the loan.[32] In light of the unemployment and economic stagnation that had beset the city, this delay gave rise to sharp criticism of the government's attitude to Nablus and to the hardships of its citizens.[33] Moreover, grants transferred by the government to municipal treasuries — under the aegis of transfers from royal funds and from the Point Four fund for construction and development projects in Jordanian cities — reflected a preference for East Bank municipalities, and did not promote an atmosphere of trust in the central administration by Nablus leaders.[34]

With the economic system of Nablus based to a considerable degree on domestic trade, the removal of all restrictions on movement from west to east across the Jordan River on 14 November 1949 was of great significance. On 1 December of that year customs on goods crossing the river were also abolished.[35] In addition, Nablus benefited from the paving and widening of the Damyah–al-Salt road in 1949 and 1950 and the Nablus–Damyah road in 1952.[36] With the completion of these projects, the inhabitants and the merchants of Nablus had at their disposal a 70-kilometer paved road that linked them directly to Amman.

While these measures were adopted to improve the town's economy, whether directly or indirectly, they were far from enough to satisfy the local population. Frustrated expectations were to result in pressure and struggle vis-à-vis the government by various groups in Nablus during the years that followed. Yet even as early as 1949–53, relations with the government were characterized by a sense of deprivation and discrimination in Nablus. This feeling, elicited by the government's policy on import licensing, its attitude toward unemployment, and its inconsistent approach to municipal development and piecework projects, was reinforced by governmental positions on other matters as well. First, the transfer of government offices from Nablus to Jerusalem and Amman frustrated the ambitions of the city leaders to turn Nablus into "the primary [urban] center among the cities of the kingdom after the capital,"[37] that is, to turn it into the capital of the West Bank. The policy of concentrating the West Bank administration in Jerusalem aroused a wave of protest in the city in July and August 1949,[38] especially over the transfer of the education department to Jerusalem.[39] However, when the government contemplated moving the trade and industry department from Jerusalem to Amman, the Nablus chamber of commerce demanded that it be left where it was.[40]

A second cause for resentment was the refusal of the Ministry of Education to help the local college (*Kuliyyat al-najah al-wataniyya*) overcome the budgetary problems it experienced in 1951 and 1952 when the waqf curtailed its regular contribution, which created great bitterness among prominent townsmen who had nurtured this educational institution since the end of the First World War.[41] Third, the Nablus public was especially outraged by the property tax assessments for 1952.[42] In addition to sending telegrams and protests to Amman and holding urgent convocations of the chamber of commerce and the city council, the property owners in the town tried to enlist the support of the press in their efforts to have the assessments canceled or reduced.[43] Fourth, the city's merchants protested forcefully against the ban imposed in June 1949 on the export of goods from the northern region of the West Bank, one of a series of orders halting the export of agricultural and industrial products issued from time to time in order to decrease inflationary pressures on the West Bank. The explanation given by the regional governor, Ahmad al-Khalil, that the authorities took these steps for the welfare of the population, did not satisfy the city's business community.[44]

Beyond the unanswered demands and the day-to-day friction with the authorities, what lay at the root of the deteriorating relations between the city leadership and the Hashemite regime was Jordan's national development policy, which was perceived in the early 1950s in Nablus, as in other West Bank towns, as favoring the East Bank by virtue of the allocation of a growing proportion of state resources to it. Toward the end of July 1952 the city's parliamentary delegates invited the 20 West Bank delegates to an emergency meeting, attended by 15 of the delegates, where a sharply worded memorandum was formulated and addressed to the prime minister. The memorandum accused the government, among other things, of adopting a double standard regarding the location of development projects and directing most investment — both government and foreign — to the East Bank.[45]

Some of the city leaders' claims may have indeed run counter to overall economic policy, as, for example, the demand to establish import quotas side by side with the demand to enlarge import license quotas. Moreover, the leaders were not always willing to understand that the ability of the government to find solutions to economic problems, such as unemployment, was limited, in view of the wider refugee problem and the separation of the West Bank from the Israeli market. Nevertheless, the claim about the concentration of development efforts on the East Bank was correct, and soon after the extension of Hashemite rule over the West Bank it was understood in Nablus that no extensive investment by the public sector could be expected. As a result, investors among the local economic elite who owned large tracts of land and who were also merchants and manufacturers began, together with the city council and the chamber of commerce, to take the initiative in developing the city's economy. This phenomenon, first manifested in the period under discussion,[46] became one of the characteristic features of the Nablus economy from the latter half of the 1950s until the war of 1967.

A MODERATE SHIFT IN THE GOVERNMENT'S ATTITUDE

While no qualitative change occurred in Hashemite policy on the economic development of Nablus, a moderate shift of emphasis in a number of spheres did become evident during the years 1954–56. An example of this shift was the establishment of a vegetable oil factory in the city. Although the government had agreed in December 1953 to acquire shares worth JD 30,000 in this venture in response to the initiative of a group of merchant-manufacturers in Nablus, including the 'Anabtawi, Masri and Shak'a families, who had undertaken to set up a plant for refining vegetable oils and producing margarine,[47] it was only in February 1955 that Tawfiq Abu al-Huda's government gave its assent in principle to granting a 30-year concession for the enterprise. The founders of the factory were also given assurances that the machinery they imported from abroad for the operation of the plant would be exempt from customs duties. In addition, the government undertook to control the import of edible oils, prohibit the establishment of competing plants, restrict the export of raw materials required for the production process, and facilitate export of the finished product after the demands of the local market had been met.[48] However, Minister of Economics Khalusi al-Khayri, who supported the

43

establishment of the Nablus factory, encountered great difficulties in obtaining final approval for the grant of the concession and the official registration of the company. A group of Jordanian ministers and delegates headed by Minister of Justice Haza' al-Majali were opposed to giving the concession to the Nablus group, as they wished to establish the plant on the East Bank or at least be allowed to set up competing plants. They appealed against the government decision, claiming that the concession was in contravention of clause 117 of the constitution, which forbade the creation of a monopoly.[49] The economics ministry countered that the government had granted a similar concession to the Jordanian Cement Factories Company, which had been formally registered by the Ministry of Justice, but this was to no avail. Haza' al-Majali and his supporters in the government blocked the concession.[50] It was only in February 1956, a month after Samir al-Rifa'i's government had been formed — without al-Majali and his supporters — that the Nablus investors succeeded in gaining final government approval for the concession and legal registration of the company. The government also acquired shares worth JD 40,000 and assisted in the sale of additional shares worth JD 90,000 to the private sector.[51]

There was also limited improvement in relations between the government and the municipality during this period. Work on expanding and improving the city's water and electricity systems, which was financed by government-guaranteed loans totaling JD 100,000 from the Ottoman Bank, reached its peak.[52] The government also approved, without excessive delay, an additional loan of JD 100,000 for a new electricity grid in the city in 1954.[53] However, in 1955, when the municipality requested government approval and a guarantee for an additional loan of JD 30,000 to complete the municipal water project, Amman refused on the grounds that the city had already undertaken heavy commitments and was incapable of assuming additional ones.[54] Moreover, the interior and finance ministries also reduced the share of revenues from fuel and other taxes transferred to the city's account that same year.[55] The municipality, as a result, found itself in a financial crisis over the implementation of its development works.

A slight improvement in the government's attitude toward the unemployment problem was evident during the years 1954–56. The Public Works Department in Nablus began to employ several hundred jobless men in road repair and paving in 1954. Carpentry shops and repair workshops for machines and motor vehicles were built in the city and in several surrounding villages, intended not only to create jobs for the unemployed but to train workers as well.[56] However, this activity lacked consistency and long-term planning, with the result that the workshops were periodically closed down by the authorities and the roadwork projects were often halted.[57]

The first all-government enterprise to be established in Nablus was the construction of grain silos that were intended to serve the entire West Bank. This was part of a broad Ministry of Agriculture plan to stock a minimum of 35,000 tons of grain throughout the country.[58] A decision was made in November 1955 to build the silos in Kafr Balata, a village bordering on the city. Construction took several months, and by the beginning of 1956 the silos began to serve the West Bank population.[59]

However, direct government investment in agriculture in the rural periphery around the city was sparse during the years under review, although the government continued to assist farmers in various ways as had been done in the past. A system of financing loans to fellahin at low interest rates was developed. Agricultural cooperatives that had operated in various villages during the Mandate were reactivated and new cooperatives were founded in other villages. A total of 20 cooperatives operated in the Nablus region, granting loans at a yearly interest rate that fluctuated between 3 and 9 percent.[60] The Development Council transferred over JD 65,000 in loan funds to these cooperatives in 1956.[61] The Ministry of Agriculture continued to extend loans to the villages through the Agricultural Bank and the Point Four program.[62] Sometimes the government approved loans for specific projects, such as the development of irrigation networks in Ghur al-Far'a and Ghur al-Jiftlik.[63] Nevertheless, the Nablus merchants continued to be an important source of short-term loans for local farmers, at an interest rate that reached 30 percent a year or more.[64]

Other development plans for the countryside projected by the Ministries of Agriculture and Labor were never implemented.[65] The little that was accomplished, whether through the initiative and self-financing of the villagers or with the assistance of Point Four experts,[66] did not constitute a solution to the ongoing economic problems that burdened the rural population from the days of the Mandatory administration onward. For example, a shortage of drinking water in the summer months was not alleviated, difficulties in marketing agricultural products persisted, and there was no improvement in communication or transportation between the villages and Nablus.[67]

The slight improvement discernible in the attitude of the central government toward the economic development of Nablus in the years 1954–56 apparently stemmed from three developments in the Jordanian economy during the years under review: (1) the growth of the migratory movement from the West Bank to the oil economies of the Persian Gulf; (2) the growing deficit in the current account; and (3) the channeling of most government resources earmarked for economic development to the East Bank.

Emigration from the West Bank to the oil-producing Arab states began mounting in the second half of 1952, reaching several thousand persons each month in 1955–56. The official position on this population movement was ambivalent from the outset. On the one hand, the government assumed — rightly — that the emigrants would send remittances to their families who had stayed behind on the West Bank, thereby contributing to a reduction in the size of the deficit in the current account. Moreover, the government regarded emigration as an important means of reducing the scale of overt unemployment on the West Bank. On the other hand, however, it feared that continued emigration of the size and nature as had been taking place since the latter half of 1952 would exacerbate the shortage of skilled manpower and thus hinder the implementation of development projects as well as ongoing economic activity. Thus, while the government took steps to facilitate the absorption of Jordanian nationals in the Arab oil economies,[68] it simultaneously began in 1955 to monitor and control the migratory movement through the selective granting of exit permits. In May 1955, for example, the emigration of doctors, pharmacists and midwives to Kuwait was prohibited; civil servants who wished to emigrate required the approval of their superiors; and interior ministry officials placed obstacles in the path of engineers, technicians and other skilled workers in various fields who wished to leave Jordan.[69]

Not surprisingly, this policy elicited complaints from West Bank residents.[70] A more basic means available to the government for reducing the emigration rate was through the initiation of, or assistance to, development projects in high-unemployment areas on the West Bank. To a limited extent this was done in Nablus, where emigration had a strong impact. In August 1956 *Filastin* reported that businessmen in the city were complaining about the shortage of craftsmen and skilled workers,[71] a consequence of emigration. It was this trend which apparently contributed to the governmental decisions to finance the construction of the vegetable oil factory, approve loans to the city council, expand the range of municipal services, and improve and enlarge the scope of public works projects in and around Nablus.

Deficit in the current account had characterized the Jordanian economy even before the annexation of the West Bank. However, after the 1948 war and the annexation, the absolute and relative size of the deficit reached extremely high proportions by any standard. In 1950–52 the overall import surplus exceeded total imports by 70 percent or more,[72] prompting the government to seek ways of increasing exports and decreasing imports. Although a comprehensive policy for reducing the deficit in the current account had not yet been formalized in the period under review, the government did take several steps in this direction. One of them was passing the Law to Promote and Direct Industry, in May 1955, which was aimed, inter alia, at encouraging the establishment of industrial enterprises that would produce import substitutes. The law assured new industrial enterprises easy terms for tax payment and tax exemptions on imported equipment. One of the industries that the government wished to encourage in this way was the edible oil industry, named explicitly in the law itself,[73] which accounted for the aid — financial and other — eventually given by the government to establish the vegetable oil factory in Nablus.

The Jordanian government increased overall development expenditure during the early 1950s from JD 801,000 in 1950 to over JD 4 million by 1954, with total development expenditure during the years 1950–54 amounting, in current prices, to JD 10.2 million.[74] As a consequence of economic and political considerations, however, the major portion of these resources was earmarked by the government for the development of the East Bank. This policy antagonized the West Bank population toward the Hashemite regime. With Nablus being one of the main political centers on the West Bank, and the positions of its leaders carrying great weight among the Palestinian population throughout the kingdom, the government monitored public opinion in the city closely. It would appear, therefore, that the modest changes in the allocation of state resources for the development of Nablus in 1954–56 resulted from an understanding in Amman that, considering the sizable investment being made in the East Bank, the needs and expectations of the population in the West Bank

47

ought not be completely ignored. This attitude may at least partially explain the fact that of the four industrial companies established with government investment during the period under discussion, one, at least, was situated on the West Bank — Jordan Vegetable Oil Industries Company in Nablus (see table 2.1).

Table 2.1.
Jordanian government shareholdings in four major companies, 1954/55[a]
(in JD)

	Authorized capital	Paid-up capital	Amount subscribed by government
Jordan Phosphate Mines Co.	1,000,000	409,130	250,000
Jordan Cement Factories Co.	1,000,000	1,000,000	495,000
Jordan Vegetable Oil Industries Co.	200,000	130,000	40,000
Jordan Fisheries Co.	100,000	50,000	10,000
Total	2,300,000	1,589,130	795,000

Note: a   Fiscal year.
Source: IBRD, *Jordan*, 1957, p. 237.

CONCLUSION

A pattern of relations developed between the government and the population and leadership of Nablus during the first eight years of Hashemite rule over the West Bank which, to some extent, characterized the regime's economic relationship with the entire West Bank. This pattern, which continued to shape the economic relationship between Nablus and the regime until June 1967, had a dual foundation. On the one hand, after a lengthy period of low rates of economic growth as a result of the political instability in Palestine at the end of the Mandatory period, the Nablus economy faced a new economic and social situation — severance from the Jewish economy, and the influx of tens of thousands of refugees — for which it was unprepared and which caused a serious crisis. The annexation of the West Bank to the Hashemite Kingdom at this time raised expectations in Nablus of a rapid improvement in economic conditions and rescue from the crisis it faced. On the other hand, the government initially lacked the

48

tools and resources to contend with the economic problems that accompanied annexation. Even subsequently, when the scope of the resources at its disposal was expanded, it designated the rapid development of the East Bank as its chief economic priority, with the development of the West Bank assuming only secondary importance.

Relations between the government and the city of Nablus passed through two stages: the first (1949–53) was characterized by the frustration of hopes for an economic breakthrough under the Hashemite regime and a sense of alienation and hostility on the part of the population toward it; the second (1954–56) was marked by the government's attempt to moderate this resentment by allotting limited funds for the development of the city.

This pattern produced three results in terms of the city's economy during the period under study and thereafter. First, Nablus growth rates were lower than those of most of the major cities on the East Bank. Second, emigration from the town to the Arab oil-producing states, which began as a flight from unemployment and economic hardship, became, in the late 1950s and 1960s, a major stimulus for growth in Nablus, with the migrants' remittances to their families back home serving, inter alia, as the principal source of investment in the construction industry, crafts and services. Third, the public sector's meager initiative in Nablus motivated the private sector, and in particular the local economic elite, to invest in the development of the city. This trend, discernible in the early 1950s, became even more pronounced in the 1960s. Private sector initiative was also made possible by the traditional presence in Nablus of enterpreneurs, a presence dating back to the period of Ottoman rule at the end of the nineteenth century.

The economic relationship between Nablus and the Hashemite regime also had political aspects. Most of the city's leaders belonged to the camp that had opposed the Husaynis in the Mandate period, and some of them had participated in the political activity that installed Hashemite rule in the West Bank. However, during the 1950s the city became one of the foci of opposition to the regime. It was an important base of the Communist, the Ba'th and the Qawmiyyun al-'Arab Parties, and its citizens played an active role in the widespread riots of 1955–56 which threatened the very existence of the regime. These developments stemmed in part from frustration and disappointment with the economic policies of the government, along with growing socioeconomic tensions within the city itself.

A part of the local elite, however, continued to support the Hashemite regime, as the government was wise enough to channel most of the funds allotted to Nablus through this group. Moreover, under Hashemite rule new opportunities opened up for the Nablus elite to expand their economic activities on the East Bank. This complexity in the relations between the population of Nablus and the Hashemites was to characterize the city until June 1967 and even thereafter, when totally different factors and conditions would determine its economic development.

NOTES

1. *Filastin*, 10 August, 20 September 1949, 28 February, 26, 13 June 1950; *al-Difa'*, 9 August 1949, 26 June 1950.
2. *Filastin*, 24 December 1949. Cf. *al-Jihad*, 28 December 1953.
3. *al-'Urdun*, 6 August 1949; *al-Difa'*, 7 August 1949; Hikmat al-Masri in an interview with the author, 8 December 1967.
4. *al-'Urdun*, 6 August 1949.
5. *Filastin*, 27 June 1950; *al-Difa'*, 27 June 1950; *al-'Urdun*, 27 January 1950.
6. See memorandum to the Minister of Commerce and Industry, *Filastin*, 3 May 1950.
7. *Filastin*, 4 September, 24 December 1949, 28 February, 20 April 1950.
8. DS, *SY 1953*, p. 2.
9. *Filastin*, 19 February 1950.
10. *al-Difa'*, 13 April 1950.
11. *Filastin*, 30 June, 30 July, 23 August 1949.
12. Ibid., 29 October 1950.
13. *al-Difa'*, 30 November 1950; *Filastin*, 7 February, 7, 9 March, 4 April 1951.
14. *al-Difa'*, 18 November 1951; *al-Bilad*, 25 February 1952.
15. *Filastin*, 30 April 1950.
16. See, e.g., ibid., 15 April 1952, 27 August, 1953; *al-Jihad*, 29 December 1953.
17. *Filastin*, 29 August 1953.
18. Ibid., 14 February 1949, 6 June, 20 February 1951, 8 March 1952; *al-Difa'*, 26 November 1951.
19. *Filastin*, 19 October 1949, 24 March, 9 May, 4 June, 10 December 1950, 11, 12, 14, 22 February, 4, 28 March, 18, 25, 29 April 1951, 21 March, 13 July, 12 August 1952; *al-Difa'*, 9 August, 19 October 1949; *al-Bilad*, 11 August 1952; *al-Jihad*, 31 December 1953.
20. See, e.g., *Filastin*, 27 March 1952.
21. Ibid., 26 January, 22 March 1951, 12 August 1952; *al-Bilad*, 11 August 1952.
22. *al-Jihad*, 28, 31 December 1953.
23. *Filastin*, 14, 22 February 1951.
24. Ibid., 30 April 1950.
25. Ibid., 12, 14, 24 March, 20 April 1950, 3 March, 20 June 1951.
26. Ibid., 16 July 1952.
27. *al-'Urdun*, 8 May 1950.
28. *al-Jihad*, 27 December 1953.
29. *Filastin*, 30 June 1949, 4 June 1950; *al-Bilad*, 7 April 1952.
30. *Filastin*, 4 June 1950, 14 February 1951.
31. Ibid., 30 April, 5 May, 27 October, 1950; *al-Difa'*, 22 August 1950, 9 December 1951.

32. *Filastin,* 7 March, 8 April 1952.
33. Qadri Tuqan in an interview with the author, 12 January 1968.
34. *Filastin,* 27 April 1950; *al-Difa',* 3 November 1952.
35. *al-Difa',* 21 November 1949; *al-'Urdun,* 1, 2 December 1949.
36. *al-'Urdun,* 15 September 1949; *al-Bilad,* 7 April 1952.
37. *Filastin,* 30 April 1950. Cf. *al-'Urdun,* 6 August 1949.
38. "Current Affairs," *Hamizrah Hehadash* 1 (1950): 61; Qadri Tuqan in an interview with the author, 13 January 1968.
39. *al-Difa',* 26 July 1949.
40. *Filastin,* 2, 10 February 1950.
41. Ibid., 29 June 1951; Qadri Tuqan in an interview with the author, 13 January 1968.
42. *Filastin,* 30 June, 14 August, 20 October, 24 December 1949, 4 April 1951.
43. Ibid., 4, 21 March 1952. Cf. ibid., 15 April 1952.
44. Ibid., 11 June 1949; *al-'Urdun,* 27 July 1949. Cf. *Filastin,* 18 February, 1 March 1949.
45. *al-Hayat,* 2 August 1952.
46. *Filastin,* 24 April 1952.
47. See above, p. 40.
48. *Filastin,* 10 February 1955.
49. Ibid., 10 May 1955.
50. Ibid., 11 December 1955.
51. Ibid., 29 February 1956. Cf. ibid., 10 February and 2 July 1955.
52. Ibid., 9 June 1954; *al-Difa',* 9 June 1954.
53. *Filastin,* 3, 6 October, 3 November 1954; *al-Jihad,* 3 October 1954.
54. *Filastin,* 13, 26 July 1955; *al-Difa',* 12, 13 July, 28 August 1955.
55. *al-Difa',* 24 March 1955; *Filastin,* 24 March, 26 July 1955.
56. *Filastin,* 25 March, 3 July, 2 November 1954; *al-Jihad,* 2 November 1954; *al-Difa',* 12 September 1955.
57. *Filastin,* 1 May 1955; *al-Difa',* 11 December 1955.
58. *al-Difa',* 21 November, 18 December 1955.
59. *Filastin,* 4 February, 24 June 1956.
60. Ibid., 24 July 1954; *al-Difa',* 11 December 1955.
61. *Filastin,* 30 September 1956.
62. Ibid., 21 September 1954, 24 June 1956.
63. Ibid., 30 September 1956.
64. Kazem al-Masri in an interview with the author, 18 January 1968. Cf. *al-Difa',* 8 October 1954; *Filastin,* 24 April, 3 August 1956.
65. *Filastin,* 11 December 1954, 5 April 1955; *al-Jihad,* 11 December 1954; *al-Difa',* 8 December 1955.
66. *Filastin,* 19 September, 6 November 1954, 14 July 1955, 8 July, 7 September 1956; *al-Difa',* 26 February 1956.
67. *Filastin,* 29 September 1954, 12 June 1955, 26 January 1956; *al-Difa',* 14 July, 4 November 1955, 27 February 1956.
68. E.g., the government conducted lengthy negotiations with the Kuwaiti authorities to abolish entry visas and worked to mitigate discrimination against the migrants in wages and work conditions. See *Filastin,* 13 January, 30 April 1954; *al-Difa',* 8 January, 12 March 1954, 18 July 1955; *al-Jihad,* 3 February 1954.
69. *al-Jihad,* 10 May 1955; Kazem al-Masri in an interview with the author, 18 January 1968.
70. *al-Jihad,* 21 June 1955; *Filastin,* 22 June 1955.
71. *Filastin,* 25 August 1956. Cf. ibid., 18 May, 20 July 1954.
72. IBRD, *Jordan,* pp. 461–62.
73. *al-Jarida al-rasmiyya al-'urduniyya,* 1 May 1955.
74. IBRD, *Jordan,* p. 469.

3

Demographic and Economic
Origins of the Intifada

INTRODUCTION

"A drowning man is not worried about getting wet." While the inclusion of this Arabic saying in the first leaflet distributed by the Islamic Resistance Movement in the Gaza Strip in December 1987 at the beginning of the Intifada[1] was probably not intended as a reference to the prevailing economic situation in the territories under Israeli occupation, the saying certainly could be applied to the economic crisis which had plagued the residents of these territories for a long time before the uprising began.

In examining the causes and manifestations of the economic crisis in the West Bank and the Gaza Strip, including relevant demographic developments, it is important to emphasize that there is no a priori relationship between this crisis and the outbreak of the Intifada. However, the extent to which the ongoing economic crisis contributed to the outbreak and continuation of the Intifada must be assessed.

Before the Intifada, the CBS was able to collect data in the occupied territories in a fairly wide range of social, economic and demographic areas. These were published in the CBS annual report (*Statistical Abstract of Israel*) and in special publications on the occupied territories (*Statistical Quarterly for the Administered Areas*, 1973–81; *Statistics of Judea, Samaria and the Gaza District*, 1982–87). The figures in these publications have been extensively cited, serving as the basis for research in Israel and abroad and are widely referred to in PLO publications.[2] CBS statistics are considered reliable, and the Bureau has a proven record in maintaining its distance from the debates and divisions within Israeli society on the question of the territories. Still, unrelated to the political debate, questions have been raised regarding the accuracy of CBS statistics, especially demographic ones. It was claimed that the September 1967 West Bank census (the only one conducted in the territories under Israeli rule) undercounted the population, as it was carried out only three months after the June war, before the Israeli administration in the West Bank had a chance to fully establish itself. Other factors contributing to this inaccuracy were lack of cooperation on the part of the Palestinian population with the CBS census-takers, and the failure to count residents who were temporarily out of the country. For these reasons, a significant proportion of the population may not have been included in the 1967 census. According to a rather high estimate, the undercount in the census could have amounted to an additional 200,000–300,000 people by 1987.[3] Another area cited in connection with claims of undercounting is the number of Palestinians from the territories who were employed in Israel in the months preceding the Intifada.[4] Nevertheless, the analysis of demographic and economic developments in this chapter is based on the CBS figures, since they are the most reliable data available.

POPULATION GROWTH

The year 1982 marked a significant change in the rate of population growth in the West Bank. The seven preceding years (1975–81), had witnessed an extremely low rate of annual population growth — between 0.8 and 1.8 percent, or an average of 1.3 percent (see table 1.6), representing an increment of 56,600 to the West Bank Palestinian population in that period. Following these "seven lean years" were six years (1982–87) of relatively high increase rates: 2.4–3.0 percent annually, or an average of 2.7 percent, more than double the figure for the previous period (table 1.6). This represented an addition of 128,000 to the West Bank Palestinian population, 2.3 times greater than the increase between 1975 and 1981.

Two developments help to explain this change: a rise in the rate of natural increase and a net fall in migration. The change in both these demographic variables began in 1982. The rise in natural increase rates was moderate — from an annual average of 32.0 per thousand in 1975–81 to an average of 33.6 per thousand

53

in 1982–86 (see table 1.7). This change can be attributed to a steep decline in the death rate combined with a less dramatic fall in the birthrate. The average annual death rate fell from 12.2 per thousand in 1977–79 to 8.3 per thousand in 1984–86, representing a decrease of 32 percent within a very short period. At the same time, the average annual birthrate fell from 44.3 to 41.1 per thousand, a decrease of only 7.2 percent.[5] The phenomenon of a steeper fall in the death rate than in the birthrate was not unique to the West Bank during this period. It was common in other Islamic Middle Eastern societies in the 1970s and 1980s, a result of various aspects of the modernization process. Mortality rates fall sharply following an improvement in health and sanitation services and overall living conditions, whereas the fall in the birthrate is attributable to longer-term economic, social and cultural changes whose impact is felt only after several generations. In absolute terms, the rise in the rate of natural increase meant an annual addition of 22–23,000 to the total Palestinian population in the West Bank in 1977–79, compared with over 27,000 in 1984–86.

The second development that affected the growth of the West Bank Palestinian population was the slowing of the eastward migration from the West Bank. According to CBS data, in 1975–81, the peak income-producing years for the Arab oil-exporting states, the net migration balance exceeded 10,000 annually. The demand for workers in those states, and the tempting salaries in almost all fields of employment, proved a powerful magnet for West Bank inhabitants. During 1979–81 in particular, when the demand for skilled and unskilled workers was at its highest point, net departures to the Arab oil countries amounted to 45,600 persons, or about 66 percent of the total rise in population due to natural increase (69,400) for those years. However, in 1982 the oil economies began to slump, and income from oil exports in Kuwait, Saudi Arabia and the United Arab Emirates plunged. In Saudi Arabia alone, oil export revenues dropped from $113 billion in 1981 to $20 billion in 1986, representing a fall of about 84 percent at current prices.[6] The drop in income led to a drop in investments, with a correspondingly steep fall in the demand for foreign workers, including those from the West Bank. The slowdown quickly affected the non-oil economies, including Jordan, which also experienced a decline in the demand for West Bank workers. From 1982 onward, many workers who were dismissed or whose contracts had expired returned home.

The data reveal the depth of the economic depression: in 1983 the net migration balance amounted to only 2,700 persons, and in the following three years, 1984–86, the total was only 15,900 (see table 1.7). For those years, net migration equaled 19 percent of the total rise in population due to natural increase (81,800).

Demographic growth in the Gaza Strip from the first half of the 1970s until 1987 resembled that of the West Bank, although the pace of change was more moderate. There as well, 1982 marked a turning point in the rate of population growth. From 1975 to 1981, the average annual population growth rate was a high 2.8 percent rising even higher, to 3.4 percent, in 1982–87. Population growth in the Gaza Strip in the six years prior to the Intifada totaled 95,200, a figure that does not include about 7,000 persons from the Rafah area, which was returned to Egypt in 1982. This growth must be compared with an increase of about 73,000 in 1975–81, including the al-'Arish area which was returned to Egypt in 1979 (see table 1.6).

Like the West Bank, the Gaza Strip experienced a rise in the rate of natural increase in the years preceding the Intifada. In 1984, the natural increase rate among the Palestinian population in the Gaza Strip exceeded 40.0 per thousand for the first time. Two years later, in 1986, a similar rate was recorded. The average annual rate of natural increase in 1982–86 reached 38.8, compared with 37.0 in 1975–81 (see table 1.7). As in the West Bank, the rise is attributable mainly to the steep decline in the death rate. The average annual death rate fell from 11.0 per thousand in 1977–79 to 7.6 per thousand in 1984, representing a decrease of about 31 percent, similar to that recorded in the West Bank during this period. At the same time, the average annual birthrate declined slightly, from 47.7 to 47.1 per thousand.[7] These extremely high birth and natural increase rates in the 1980s are not found in other Palestinian populations for which demographic data are available. For example, among Muslims in Israel, for whom the highest rates of natural increase were recorded in the 1960s, the average annual rate of natural increase reached 30.9 per thousand in 1985–87 (see table 1.4).

Migration from the Gaza Strip never reached substantial proportions, even in the boom years in Jordan and the Arab oil states. Net migration in 1979–81 amounted to 15,200 people, with a decrease following the slowdown which hit the Arab oil economies. In 1984–86, the net number of departures from the Gaza Strip to those states was 11,300 (see table 1.7), a figure

55

equal to 18 percent of the total rise in population due to natural increase (61,800).

One result of the rise in the rate of natural increase and the fall in migration was the high proportion of young people within the West Bank and Gaza Strip population. In 1987, about 70 percent of the total population in the territories was younger than 25 years, with the proportion of those aged 45 and above amounting to only 13 percent (see table 3.1). The slowing of migration after 1981 led to an increase in the relative share of the 20–24 and 25–29 age groups, a development that was particularly noticeable in the West Bank.

In addition to these demographic changes, the 1970s and 1980s witnessed a period of far-reaching changes in the field of education in the West Bank and the Gaza Strip. Both the public and private sectors, each for its own reasons and motives, invested in expanding the educational system in the West Bank and the Gaza Strip. There was a distinct rise in the demand for secondary and higher education during the 15 years preceding the Intifada. Many young people were propelled toward secondary and higher education by the low alternative cost in the territories on the one hand, and the great demand for high school and university graduates in the oil economies on the other. The fact that there was a broad geographical distribution of universities and colleges

Table 3.1

West Bank and Gaza Strip: population estimates by age, 1987

Age	West Bank		Gaza Strip	
	thousands	percent	thousands	percent
Total	868.1	100.0	565.6	100.0
0–4	170.2	19.7	115.6	20.4
5–14	238.6	27.5	160.9	28.4
15–19	90.5	10.4	58.8	.10.4
20–24	89.5	10.3	53.9	9.5
25–34	122.2	14.0	78.5	13.9
35–44	44.6	5.1	33.9	5.9
45–54	42.0	4.8	26.2	4.7
55–64	38.4	4.5	22.1	4.0
65+	32.1	3.7	15.7	2.8

Source: CBS, *SAI 1989*, p. 701, table 27/2.

in the territories further facilitated the increase in enrollment at institutions of higher education.[8]

The results of these developments are remarkable: the percentage of the population with elementary, secondary and higher education rose sharply in the 1970s and 1980s. In 1970, among the population aged 14 and over, only 16 percent had nine years of education or more in the West Bank, and 25 percent in the Gaza Strip. By 1987, these rates had risen to 38 percent and 49 percent respectively. For the total male population aged 14 and above, the relative share of those with post-elementary education reached 48 percent in the West Bank and 54 percent in the Gaza Strip for the same year. The increase in the rates of secondary and higher education was even more pronounced: in 1970, only 1 percent of the total population aged 14 and above in the territories had completed 13 years of education or more. By 1987, this figure had jumped to 11 percent in the West Bank and 10 percent in the Gaza Strip (see table 3.2).

Taking into account the age breakdown of the West Bank and Gaza Strip populations, these changes meant that tens of thousands of young people had acquired secondary and higher education. In 1987, of about 247,000 West Bank Palestinians aged 18–34, there were 89,000 with 9–12 years of education and 41,000 with 13 years or more. For the same age group in Gaza, out of a total of 154,000, there were 72,000 who had 9–12 years of

Table 3.2

West Bank and Gaza Strip: proportion of population aged 14 and over by years of schooling, 1970 and 1987
(in percentages)

	1970		1987	
	9+	13+	9+	13+
West Bank				
Total	16	1	38	11
Males	23	1	48	14
Gaza Strip				
Total	25	0.5	49	10
Males	32	1	54	15

Source: CBS, *SAI 1988*, pp. 752–53, table 27/46.

education and about 25,000 who had 13 years or more. Thus, when the Intifada began, there were about 66,000 Palestinians (44,000 men and 22,000 women) aged 18–34 in the West Bank and Gaza Strip who had acquired at least a high school education (see table 3.3). If we add those aged 35 and above with post-secondary education, the number of people in the West Bank and Gaza Strip with 13 years of education or more exceeded 81,000.

High education rates continued even after the demand for skilled workers and university graduates in the Arab oil economies fell off. About 16,000 students registered for the 1986/87 school year at universities and colleges in the West Bank and Gaza Strip, while about 165,000 pupils registered at elementary and secondary schools in the fall of 1987.[9]

Table 3.3
*West Bank and Gaza Strip: male population aged 14 and over
by years of schooling and age, 1987*
(in percentages)

Age	Total (thousands)	Years of Schooling		
		7–8	9–12	13+
			(percent of total)	
West Bank				
Total	221.3	14.7	34.2	13.9
15–17	27.0	22.6	62.2	(0.4)
18–24	66.0	15.9	46.0	20.6
25–34	61.3	17.9	33.1	21.3
35–44	17.2	13.9	27.7	12.7
45–54	18.5	(7.5)	11.8	(6.5)
55–64	16.3	(4.9)	4.9	(1.8)
65+	14.4	2.1	(1.4)	(0.7)
Gaza Strip				
Total	137.0	9.3	39.8	14.6
15–17	16.4	13.4	66.5	(0.6)
18–24	41.0	11.2	44.3	20.8
25–34	39.1	10.5	41.9	21.7
35–44	12.8	5.5	49.2	15.6
45–54	11.1	(5.4)	20.5	(6.3)
55–64	9.7	(3.1)	(4.1)	(2.1)
65+	6.9	(1.5)	(1.5)	—

Source: CBS, *SAI 1988*, pp. 752–53, table 27/46.

58

ECONOMIC RECESSION

The early 1980s also marked a clear change in economic development in the West Bank and Gaza Strip. While during the 1970s the territories had enjoyed high rates of economic growth, the pace of growth slowed greatly from 1981–82 onward.

In 1970–75 the average annual GNP growth rate in the territories reached a high of 14 percent in real terms. This unprecedented growth rate resulted from two developments: the sharp rise in productivity in the agricultural sector following the introduction of new methods by the Israeli Ministry of Agriculture, and the increasing number of unemployed Palestinians who found jobs in Israel. According to CBS figures for 1975, about 35,000 workers from the West Bank (27.6 percent of the total employed labor force) and 27,000 from Gaza (35.6 percent of the total employed labor force) were working in Israel. The early 1970s were also the years of the "great leap" in the economic integration of the West Bank and Gaza Strip into the Israeli economy.[10]

This accelerated economic growth continued in the second half of the 1970s, albeit at a slower pace. Between 1975 and 1980 the rise in GNP in the West Bank and the Gaza Strip averaged 7 percent annually in real terms. This growth was caused primarily by external factors, especially remittances sent to their families by Palestinians working in Jordan and the Arab oil states, a direct outcome of the economic boom which swept the region following the steep rise in oil prices in 1973–74 and again in 1979–80. The factors which had fueled economic growth in the first half of the decade, i.e., increased agricultural productivity and income from employment in Israel, almost dried up during the second half of the decade.[11]

Growth further slowed in the 1980s, with GNP growth in 1981–82 down to 3.8 percent in the West Bank and to only 1.7 percent in the Gaza Strip. The average annual GNP growth rate during 1981–86 was 3.2 percent in the West Bank and 1.7 percent in Gaza (see table 3.4). This fall resulted from the recession in the Arab oil states and the slowdown in Jordan's economy, both of which led to a decline in total remittances by inhabitants of the territories working in these states.[12] The other factors which had contributed to rapid economic growth during the first half of the 1970s had little impact, as the Israeli economy itself was also in recession during those years. The West Bank and the Gaza Strip sank into economic stagnation during the first half of

Table 3.4
West Bank and Gaza Strip: economic indicators, 1970–86
(annual averages, in percentages)

	1970–71	1972–73	1974–75	1976–77	1977–78	1979–80	1981–82	1983–84	1985–86
West Bank and Gaza Strip									
GNP	18.0	11.0	10.5	6.5	5.7	6.7	3.1	2.4	2.5
GDP	12.0	6.0	9.5	6.5	6.2	5.9	2.0	2.0	5.6
West Bank									
GNP	17.5	9.0	12.0	6.5	5.5	6.0	3.8	2.0	3.5
GDP	11.0	6.0	11.5	7.0	6.5	6.2	3.5	2.6	6.0
Gaza Strip									
GNP	19.5	16.5	7.0	6.5	6.1	8.2	1.7	3.2	0.2
GDP	14.0	7.0	5.0	5.5	5.6	4.9	-1.9	0.0	4.4

Sources:
1970–71 to 1976–77:
Uri Litwin, *Kalkalat ha-shtahim ha-muhzakim 1976-1977*, Jerusalem: Bank of Israel — Research Department, 1980, pp. 18–20, tables 2–4.
1977–78 to 1985–86:
D. Zaka'i, pp. 23–25, table 5.

the 1980s when the two economic systems which had propelled its growth, Israel and the Arab states east of the Jordan River, floundered economically. The economies of the West Bank and the Gaza Strip were themselves too weak to continue to sustain growth, particularly in the fields of agriculture, construction and industry.

Stagnation was particularly evident in industry. The industrial component in the Palestinian economy had always been low, accounting in the early 1970s for 7-8 percent of the GDP in the West Bank and about 10 percent in Gaza. In 1985-86 its share in the GDP was the same, with employment in industry in the territories never exceeding 16 percent throughout the 1980s.[13] The causes for this stagnation were the private sector's preference for investing in trade and services; lack of investment from the public sector or from foreign investors; competition with goods manufactured in Israel; and difficulty in penetrating the Jordanian market due to that country's administrative restrictions.[14]

In the absence of growth at home, and with the reversal of the circumstances that had made possible an influx of resources from neighboring economies, the high rate of population growth acquired special significance with respect to income levels and living standards. The result was negative per capita growth rates. In 1981-85, GNP per capita fell at an average annual rate of 1.8 percent in Gaza and 0.7 percent in the West Bank. In current dollar terms, GNP per capita in Gaza dropped from $1,012 in 1981/82 to $855 in 1984/85, a decrease of about 16 percent. In the West Bank, GNP per capita during this period fell from $1,331 to $1,215, a drop of 9 percent (see table 3.5). This represented

Table 3.5

West Bank and Gaza Strip: disposable private income per capita, 1981-87
(New Israeli Shekel in 1986 prices)

	West Bank	Gaza Strip
1981	2,259.3	2,065.5
1982	2,535.4	2,031.7
1983	2,332.0	1,946.8
1984	2,251.1	1,754.1
1985	2,117.2	1,512.5
1986	2,664.7	1,698.5
1987	2,626.8	1,894.4

Source: CBS, *JSGAS*, vol. 18/2 (1988), p. 26, table 7; p. 36, table 15.

the first drop in GNP per capita in the territories since the 1967 war. Moreover, it followed a decade of steep rise in disposable per capita income. The slowdown thus represented a turnaround in economic development in the territories. Many households were affected, especially in the refugee camps, where overcrowding grew even worse, and in the lower strata of both the rural and the urban populations.[15]

A rise in unemployment was another aspect of the recession, both among skilled as well as among unskilled workers. CBS figures are incomplete, but those available indicate a significant rise in the number of job-seekers. There was also a large increase in the number of unemployed persons who did not seek work through official employment channels — estimated at about 31,000 in 1985.[16] This figure is high in relation to the absolute size of the work force in the territories. It is widely believed that many of the unemployed did not apply to the official labor bureaus because the only employment available was unskilled manual labor, primarily in construction and services in Israel, and high school and university graduates preferred to forego employment as dish-washers or sanitation workers in Israel's cities.

Many others, however, could not afford to reject employment in Israel. According to CBS figures for the summer of 1987, about 109,000 workers from the territories were employed in Israel.[17] According to other sources, the figure was even higher — between 130,000 and 140,000 workers (male and female, aged 15 and above).[18] These workers constituted a substantial share of the employed work force in the territories: about 35 percent of the total employed work force in the West Bank and 46 percent in Gaza, according to CBS figures for 1987 (see table 3.6). Since

Table 3.6
West Bank and Gaza Strip:
employed persons in Israel, 1975-87 (various years)
(in thousands)

	Total	West Bank	Gaza Strip
1975	66.3	40.4	25.9
1980	75.1	40.6	34.5
1985	89.2	47.5	41.7
1987	108.9	62.9	46.0

Source: CBS, SAI 1990, p. 729, table 27.21.

most workers from the territories were men in the 18-34 age group, the proportion of those employed in Israel from 1983-87, of the total number of workers in this age group, was indeed significant, representing the vast majority in Gaza and over half in the West Bank.

Given these high rates, the significance of the employment of Palestinians from the territories in Israel cannot be minimized. Educated men from the major towns in the territories were undoubtedly frustrated at having no alternative but to support themselves and their families at jobs which required little skill, had negative social status, and provided meager compensation. Moreover, many, if not all, Palestinians from the territories working in Israel suffered daily humiliations, including makeshift living conditions for the thousands of workers who stayed overnight in Israel, frequent security checks, and degrading treatment often meted out by employers and the public at large. Humiliation and frustration eventually gave rise to profound anger, if not hatred, toward the society that employed them under these conditions. This situation endured during 1982-87, and while many sought jobs elsewhere, the recession in the Arab oil economies and the economic stagnation in the territories forced them to continue working in Israel.

CONCLUSION

Most of the economic and demographic data show that the territories entered a period of economic recession in 1982. The outbreak of the Intifada at the end of 1987 thus came after about six years of economic recession, including two particularly difficult years, 1985 and 1986. Moreover, the fact that a decade of high economic growth and rising income and living standards had preceded the recession exacerbated the subsequent hardship.

The following developments may be singled out as the major causes, manifestations and economic effects of the recession:

(1) Deterioration in the standard of living resulting, inter alia, from the rise in the rate of population growth in the territories.

(2) An increase in the relative share of the population under the age of 15.

(3) A fall in GNP growth rate in the territories, resulting in a fall in per capita income in 1982-85.

(4) Increased overcrowding in the refugee camps in the West Bank and Gaza Strip.

(5)   A marked rise in the enrollment rate in secondary and post-secondary institutions of education.

(6)   A significant increase in the number of unemployed workers, especially among those with secondary and post-secondary education.

The extent that these demographic and economic developments were responsible for the outbreak of the Intifada and its continuation may be examined in two different contexts: along a time axis, and in terms of overall development.

Economic development along a time axis. James C. Davies has noted that societies react particularly strongly to economic recession when it follows a period of prosperity, with the reaction to recession in direct proportion to the degree of prosperity that preceded it. More than the hardship itself, it is the transition from a continual rise in income level and living standards to economic stagnation and a drop in living standards that eventually leads to resentment against the government, which is held responsible for the situation.[19] The French, Russian and Iranian revolutions, to take examples from various periods, all occurred under the conditions of recession following tangible prosperity described by Davies. Significantly, the Intifada began in Gaza, where the extent of the recession was greater than in the West Bank. The timing also corresponds with Davies' thesis concerning a necessary "maturation period" before the changed economic situation ripens into social and political action. In this case, it took about six years from the economic "breaking point" until the eruption of the Intifada. From an economic perspective, then, the early years of the recession may be viewed as the beginning of the process that led to the Intifada.

Economic development within the overall political situation. Economic factors cannot be isolated from the complex of other causes, both social and political, which led to the outbreak of the Palestinian uprising. The growing sense of frustration and anger against Israel by workers from the territories was fueled not only by economic hardship and deprivation; it was also propelled by discrimination acutely felt as an insult to individual and national pride. Economic distress thus merged with political frustration. Another example of this combination of economic and political factors can be found in the high incidence of unemployment among secondary-school and university graduates who blamed their financial distress on the Israeli government. Not only did the government refrain from encouraging local industrial development, they charged, it actively worked against them by dominating the market with the introduction of Israeli industrial goods into the territories, thus preventing or slowing local industrial initiative.

This combination of economic hardship and political oppression turned the Intifada into a protracted popular uprising, with feelings of deprivation and anger about the economic and the political situation continuing to feed on each other. Moreover, the widespread nature of the distress turned the revolt into a mass event, encompassing a variety of groups and social strata. What began as an uprising by the poor in the Gaza Strip and the West Bank, especially by residents of the refugee camps, turned into an uprising involving almost all sectors of the population.

During the late 1960s and early 1970s, the formative years of the Israeli administration in the territories, Israeli policy-makers were aware, if only intuitively, that a "dual deprivation" syndrome (economic distress and political frustration) in the territories must be avoided. Economic prosperity was intended to make the continuation of the political status quo possible.[20] In the 1980s, however, nothing was done to prevent economic crisis and hardship. The governments in power in Israel during most of the decade focused only on maintaining the political status quo in the territories, which led to the development of dual deprivation for the first time since 1967. Moreover, the governments of the 1980s barely allowed foreign governments and agencies to invest in improving the economic conditions in the West Bank and Gaza Strip. The prolongation and exacerbation of this dual deprivation were the twin pillars upon which the Intifada was founded.

NOTES

1. Leaflet [No. 1] of the Islamic Resistance Movement [Hamas], [Gaza, December 1987].
2. See especially the publications of Bank of Israel, Research Department, *The Economy of the Administered Areas, 1969... 1977*, and *Economic Development of Judea and Samaria and the Gaza District, 1981... 1986*. See also PLO, *MIF*, nos. 2–6.
3. See above, p. 14.
4. See below, p. 62.
5. Dan Zakai, *ha-Hitpathut ha-kalkalit bi-yehuda we-shomron u-ve-hevel 'azza, 1985-1986*, Jerusalem: Bank of Israel — Research Department, 1988, p. 46, table 16 (hereafter: Zakai).

6. *PE*, May 1977, June 1981, July 1989.
7. Zakai, p. 47, table 16.
8. On the development of the education system in the West Bank and Gaza Strip see Michael Winter, "Ma'arekhet ha-hinukh ba-shtahim ha-muhzaqim," in Raphael Israeli (ed.), *'Eser shnot shilton yisra'eli bi-yehuda we-shomron*, Jerusalem: Magnes Press, 1980, pp. 107-15; Sarah Graham-Brown, *Education, Repression & Liberation: Palestinians*, London: World University Service (UK), 1984, pp. 62-105; Antony Thrall Sullivan, "Palestinian Universities under Occupation," *Cairo Papers in Social Science* 11/2 (1988): p. 6-16.
9. CBS, *JSGAS*, vol. 18, no. 2 (1988), p. 299, table 1; Zakai, p. 50.
10. Rafael Meron, *ha-Hitpathut ha-kalkalit bi-yehuda we-shomron u-ve-hevel 'azza, 1970-1980*, Jerusalem: Bank of Israel — Research Department, 1982, pp. 5-14.
11. Ibid.
12. Zakai, pp. 21-22, 73.
13. CBS, *SAI 1989*, p. 707, table 27/9; p. 721, table 27/21.
14. Hisham Awartani, *A Survey of Industries in the West Bank and the Gaza Strip*, Birzeit: Birzeit University, 1979; Rose Mosleh, "al-Sina'a fi al-daffa al-gharbiyya, 1967-1979," *Shu'un Filastiniyya* 99 (1980): 4-11; Hillel Frisch, *Stagnation and Frontier: Arab and Jewish Industry in the West Bank*, Jerusalem: The West Bank Data Base Project, 1983; Simcha Bahiri, *Industrialization in the West Bank and Gaza*, Jerusalem: The West Bank Data Base Project, 1987; Bakir Abu Kishk, "Industrial Development and Policies in the West Bank and Gaza," in George T. Abed (ed.), *The Palestinian Economy*, London: Routledge, 1989, pp. 165-89.
15. See, e.g., Danny Rubinstein, "Kshemehir ha-neft yored lo qonim shemen zayit," *Davar*, 28 March 1986.
16. CBS, *JSGAS*, vol. 18, no. 2 (1988), pp. 108-9, table 4; p. 118, table 12; Zakai, pp. 50-55.
17. CBS, *JSGAS*, vol. 18, no. 2 (1988), p. 119, table 13.
18. "Employment in Israel (Palestinian)," *The West Bank Handbook*, p. 78.
19. James C. Davies, "Toward a Theory of Revolution," *American Sociological Review* 6/1 (1962): 5-19; id., "The J-Curve of Rising and Declining Satisfaction...," in Hugh Graham and Ted R. Gurr (eds.), *The History of Violence in America*, New York: Praeger, 1969, pp. 960-64.
20. Shabtai Teveth, *Qilelat ha-brakha*, Jerusalem: Schocken, 1970, pp. 285-86; Shlomo Gazit, *ha-Maqqel we-ha-gezer*, Tel Aviv: Zmore, Bitan Publishers, 1985, p. 182.

66

4

Jordan's Road to Family Planning Policy

The population of Jordan at the end of 1993, according to data published by the Jordanian authorities, was 4.152 million (see table 4.1). Forecasts prepared by the United Nations Department for Economic and Social Information indicate that by the end of the year 2000 the population of Jordan will reach 5.624 million people (see table 4.2). After years of ambiguity surrounding both the definitions and the calculations used by the Jordanian authorities, as well as by several international agencies, in estimates of the population, by the late 1980s there was no longer any doubt that official Jordanian estimates had included only the de facto population of Jordanian and foreign nationals residing in the East Bank and excluded the population of the West Bank and Jordanian citizens residing outside Jordan for long periods of time. By contrast, the population estimates of the international agencies sometimes included Jordanian citizens residing in the Persian Gulf states and inhabitants of the West Bank in their figures for Jordan.[1]

The population of Jordan grew during the 1980s, according to official estimates, at rates ranging between 3.6 percent and 4.0 percent per annum, or an annual increment of 90,000 people at the beginning of the decade (1981) to 110,000 at its close (1989). A large increase, in relative terms, occurred in the size of the Jordanian population during 1990–91 when the total population jumped from 3.111 million (end of 1989) to 3.888 million (end

Table 4.1
Jordan: population according to Jordanian, United Nations and World Bank estimates, 1961-93 (selected years)
(in thousands)

Midyear	HKJ DS	UN DESIPA	WB(1)[a]	WB(2)[b]
1961[c]	901			
1965	1,028	1,962	1,962	
1970	1,508	2,299	2,299	
1975	1,811	2,600	2,702	
1979[c]	2,133		3,126	3,100
1980	2,218	2,923	2,181	3,200
1981	2,307		2,265	3,400
1982	2,399		2,353	3,100
1983	2,495		2,446	3,200
1984	2,595		2,543	3,400
1985	2,694	3,407	2,644	3,500
1986	2,796		2,744	3,600
1987	2,897		3,846	3,800
1988	3,001		2,948	3,900
1989	3,110		3,056	3,900
1990	3,453	4,009	3,278	3,200
1991	3,888		3,664	3,700
1992	4,012			
1993	4,152			

Notes:

a   *World Tables* data.
b   *World Development Report* figures.
c   Results of Housing and Population Census.

Sources:
DS, *SY 1991*, p. 19, table 2/1; Central Bank of Jordan, Department of Research and Studies, *Monthly Statistical Bulletin* 30/5 (1994): 5; UN, DESIPA, *World Population Prospects*, The 1992 Revision, New York: UN, 1993, p. 516; WB, *World Tables 1983*, pp. 98-99; id., *World Tables 1993*, pp. 352-53; id., *World Development Report 1981...1993*; 1981-1993.

of 1991), i.e., a 25 percent increase (see table 4.1). According to Jordanian data, this increase resulted from the arrival of 540,000 returning Jordanian citizens (mostly Palestinians) and foreign nationals from Kuwait and Iraq following the Iraqi invasion of Kuwait and the eventual restoration to power of the Sabah family.

However, the official population growth estimates for 1990–91, and especially the population increase for 1991, were considered doubtful by demographers and economists in Jordan who claimed that the immigration to Jordan was grossly overestimated and that the number of returnees was lower than that published by the Department of Statistics.[2] Responding to this criticism, the authorities stood by the accuracy of the published data, claiming that they were obtained from a comprehensive survey conducted by the Department of Statistics in 1991.[3] This explanation did not dispel the doubts or defuse the claim that official estimates of 3.9 million for the total population of the Hashemite Kingdom at the end of 1991 were overestimated by at least 200,000 people. One reason for the dispute over the reliability of the official estimates was the fact that no general population census had been conducted in Jordan from 1979 until 1994. While natural population

Table 4.2
Jordan: United Nations population projections, 1991–2005
(medium-variant)

	1991–1995	1996–2000	2001–2005
Population growth rate (percent)	3.42	3.35	3.11
Crude birthrate (per thousand)	39.5	38.2	35.4
Crude death rate (per thousand)	5.5	4.8	4.3
Total fertility rate	5.7	5.3	4.8
Total Population (in millions)	4.755[a]	5.624[b]	6.572[c]

Notes:
a   Projection for 1995.
b   Projection for 2000.
c   Projection for 2005.

Source:
UN, DESIPA, *World Population Prospects*, The 1992 Revision, p. 516.

movement (births and deaths) had been recorded, and the authorities followed up developments in this regard with a reasonable degree of accuracy, the migration situation was more complicated and difficult to track in light of large-scale external migration in the 1980s.

NATURAL INCREASE

Jordan had one of the highest rates of natural increase in the world during 1980-83, averaging 37 per thousand. This rate dropped during the latter years of the 1980s and the early 1990s to 32-33 per thousand, reflecting changes in the crude birthrate. The crude birthrate, which was very high in the early 1980s — 46 per thousand on average during 1980-82 — fell to 39 per thousand in 1985 and remained at that level until 1990. Since the drop in the crude death rate was moderate — it declined from an average of 9 per thousand during 1980-82 to an average of 6.7 per thousand during 1985-91 — there was no appreciable offset of the decline in the crude birthrate (see table 4.3).

Unlike the crude birthrate and the rate of natural increase, the total fertility rate steadily declined during this period. At the start of the 1980s, the total fertility rate was 6.6 (average for 1980-82). Within several years it fell to 5.7 (average for 1989-90), and in 1991 a significantly lower rate of 5.3 was recorded.[4] A comprehensive survey on fertility and family planning (the Jordan Population and Family Health Survey), conducted by the Department of Statistics in 1990, covering 8,333 households and including interviews with 6,461 married women, reaffirmed the existence of a large gap in fertility rates between urban and rural communities in Jordan. The fertility rate of married women in large towns was 4.75 during 1988-90, while in the rural communities (including nomads) it was 6.85. The survey also reaffirmed the existence of a wide gap in fertility rates between women who had higher education and women who lacked any formal education—4.1 and 6.9 respectively.[5]

Another demographic characteristic was the wide base of the age pyramid. The percentage of the population below the age of 15 within the total population was 42.7 percent in 1991, and that of the population below the age of 20 was 55.9 percent.[6] This proportion, however, represented a decline as compared with the 1970s owing to the drop in the rate of natural increase. In 1979 the percentage of the population below the age of 15 was 50.7 percent of the total population.[7]

Table 4.3
Jordan: birthrate, death rate and natural increase rate, 1980-91
(per thousand)

	Birthrate	Death rate	Natural increase rate
1980	47	10	37
1981	46	9	37
1982	45	8	37
1983	45	8	37
1984	42	8	34
1985	39	7	32
1986	39	7	32
1987	39	7	32
1988	39	6	33
1989	39	6	33
1990	39	6	33
1991	37	5	32

Sources:
UN, ESCWA, *Demographic and Related Socio-Economic Data Sheets for Countries of the Economic Commission for Western Asia*, no. 4, Baghdad: ESCWA, 1985, p. 70, table 2; UN, *Demographic Yearbook 1984*, p. 288; *1985*, p. 515; WB, *World Development Report 1982*, p. 145, table 18; *1984*, p. 257, table 20; *1986*, p. 231, table 26; *1987*, p. 257, table 28; *1988*, p. 277, table 28; *1989*, p. 217, table 27; *1990*, p. 230, table 27; *1993*, p. 290, table 27.

The high rates of natural increase, together with the population increase brought about by the large immigration wave of 1990-91, intensified the social and economic distress that had prevailed in Jordan from the mid-1980s. The most serious consequence of this development was the inability of the Jordanian economy to supply employment to an increasingly large number of job seekers. Even before the wave of returning Palestinians to Jordan following the Iraqi invasion of Kuwait, the unemployment rate, according to Jordanian officials, was 11.5 percent.[8] This rate doubled after the end of the Gulf War, reaching 23 percent in July–September 1991, half of which was attributable to returnees from Kuwait and other countries in the Persian Gulf.[9] Some Jordanian economists claimed that the unemployment rate at the end of 1991 was in fact

Figure 4.1
Jordan: total population, 1979-92

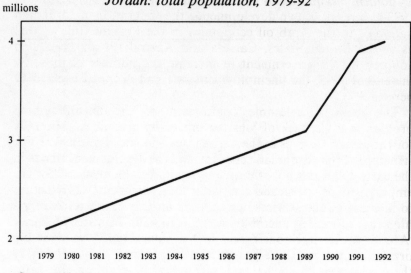

Source: table 4.1

Figure 4.2
Jordan: birthrate and death rate, 1980-91

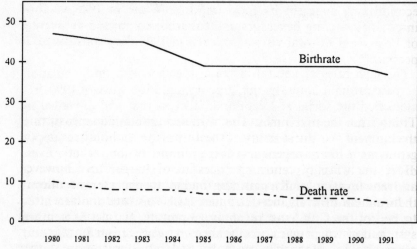

Source: table 4.3

higher than that published by the authorities, reaching as high as 35 percent.[10] The rate of unemployment, however, fell sharply in 1993 as a result of two developments: the emigration of Jordanian nationals to the Arab oil economies in the Persian Gulf as well as to the United States, Canada and Australia;[11] and measures adopted by the government to increase the number of jobs. By the end of 1993, the unemployment rate had dropped back to 11 percent.[12]

The most troublesome component of the unemployment problem was the lack of jobs for university graduates, especially for those with degrees in the humanities and social sciences.[13] The structure of the Jordanian economy and the development trends in the early 1990s did not stimulate any appreciable demand for the employment of such academics, while the government was reluctant to increase public services, which were already characterized by a high rate of hidden unemployment. Jordanian Minister of Labor 'Abd al-Karim al-Kabariti said in November 1992: "In some big organizations and some government departments, 50 percent of the employees could be laid off while maintaining the same level of productivity."[14] The authorities admitted, in light of the unexpected growth in the population in 1990–91, that "Jordan's unemployment problem is like diabetes; there is no cure, but constant treatment can keep it from getting worse."[15]

Another problem linked to the rapid increase in the population was the growing demand on food supply, leading the Jordanian economy to augment its food imports. While in 1988–90 food imports (including beverages and tobacco) comprised an average of 19 percent of total visible imports, in 1991 they constituted 26 percent.[16]

FAMILY PLANNING

The Jordanian government first initiated antinatalist measures in the early 1970s. These measures were passive and indirect, as the government did not openly encourage the use of contraceptives, nor did it supply family planning services free of charge. It did, however, allow voluntary family planning bodies to operate and allotted them a measure of financial support. It also allowed contraceptives to be imported and marketed. Furthermore, the national health system assisted couples who wished to practice family planning, especially by allowing women to undergo sterilization if they so desired. Thus, the authorities did not explicitly advocate antinatalist measures to reduce the fertility rate, but couples who wished to practice family planning did receive certain assistance from the state.[17] In terms of indirect activity, the government devoted efforts to achieving a reduction in infant mortality, as well as to improving the socioeconomic status of women.[18]

Government Measures. The beginnings of a family planning policy in Jordan date back to 1972, when the Department of Statistics initiated a conference of experts, held in Amman, to work out a population policy for the kingdom. The conference recommended that "in order to help families determine their number of offspring, family planning services should be made available in Ministry of Health clinics, other branches of government should assist by providing information, and voluntary bodies in the field should be given support."[19] Several months later, in 1973, a National Population Commission (NPC) was established under the chairmanship of the minister of labor and social development to advise the government on population issues and to promote population studies and training.[20] The authority of the NPC, however, was limited.

Over the following twenty years, the steps that the government took in implementing the antinatalist policy included the following:

(1) Provisions were made for the import and marketing of birth control devices.[21]

(2) Assistance was provided in the funding of family planning activities undertaken by voluntary organizations. The Jordanian Family Planning Association, which opened clinics in Amman and Irbid in 1972, received annual assistance from the Ministry of Social Affairs.[22]

(3) The government's own family planning services were initiated at the end of the 1970s. In 1979 the Ministry of Health began offering family planning services through the Maternal and Child Health Centers. By 1981 there were 69 such centers, and by 1985 there were about 100. These centers supplied information and guidance, focusing on the distribution of birth control pills. Only some of them could offer other types of birth control, such as the IUD.[23] The centers, however, did not actively promote the use of contraceptives: they were meant to supply a service to women and men who approached them by their own volition with a request for assistance in family planning. This approach accounts for the fact that, according to the Population and Family Health Survey of 1990, of all women who used the birth control pill as

a contraceptive, only 3.7 percent received them at the Maternal and Child Health Centers, and 8.9 percent of the women who used the IUD and 13 percent of men who used condoms received them at these centers. Out of the total users (men and women) of contraceptives, only 6.1 percent obtained them at the government's Maternal and Child Health Centers.[24]

(4) Sterilization was allowed as a legal contraceptive means. According to the Population and Family Health Survey, this was one of the most common contraceptive methods at the end of the 1980s (see table 4.4). Of the total number of women employing contraception in 1990, 21.4 percent had undergone sterilization,

Table 4.4
Jordan: trends in contraceptive use, 1976, 1983 and 1990
(percentages)

Contraceptive Method	1976[a] (N=3,455)	1983[b] (N=3,735)	1990[c] (N=6,184)
Total	100	100	100
Not using any method	77.2	74.0	65.0
Using some method[d]	22.8	26.0	35.0
Modern			
Pill	11.9	7.8	4.6
IUD	2.0	8.3	15.3
Condom	1.4	0.6	0.8
Sterilization	1.9	3.8	5.6
Other[e]	0.1	0.3	0.6
Traditional[f]			
Withdrawal	3.3	2.4	4.0
Periodic abstinence	2.1	2.9	3.9

Notes:
a   *Jordan Fertility Survey 1976.*
b   *Jordan Fertility and Family Health Survey 1983.*
c   *JPFHS 1990.*
d   Percentage of currently married women (15–49) using specific contraceptive methods.
e   Including injection and vaginal methods.
f   Prolonged breastfeeding was excluded as a contraceptive method.

Source:
JPFHS 1990, p. 39, table 4.5.

with most of the operations (73 percent) performed in government hospitals.[25]

(5) The Ministry of Health made efforts to attain religious legitimacy for the practice of family planning and the use of contraceptives both directly and through the Jordanian Family Planning Association. The ministry referred to a fatwa that had been issued by the Mufti of Jordan in December 1964 in which he stated that "the use of medicine for contraception" was allowed. He even claimed that taking drugs to cause abortion "before the embryo or the fetus is ensouled" was permitted.[26]

By the beginning of 1993, following growing demographic pressures resulting from the immigration of returnees from Kuwait and advice to the government by experts to adopt an active birth control policy, the authorities acknowledged that the government was planning to change the kingdom's population policy. Minister of Health 'Arif Batayna stated in February that "plans to universalize birth-control practices in the country are in the making."[27]

Contradictory Influences. Over the past twenty years Jordan's population policy has been the outcome of two ongoing opposing attitudes, which explains the inherent contradictions in the policy and its implementation. Three factors discouraged the adoption of an antinatalist policy:

(1) Up to the end of the 1980s Jordan was one of the smallest states in the Middle East in terms of absolute population size. In 1970 its population was 1.5 million, in 1980, 2.2 million, and in 1989, the year before the Iraqi invasion of Kuwait, 3.1 million.[28] The ruling elite in Jordan viewed the smallness of the population as a weakness and had no interest in initiating a family planning policy.

(2) Emigration, especially to the Arab oil economies in the Persian Gulf, regulated the growth of the Jordanian population. Moreover, the emigration of Palestinians and Jordanians to the oil economies not only relieved demographic pressures, it contributed to a marked increase in GNP and per capita income.[29] Thus, there were no compelling domestic forces to initiate a family planning policy. Only when emigration decreased, coupled with a large wave of immigration in the early 1990s, did the demographic factor affect the economy negatively.

(3) Jordan, like most other Islamic states, was aware that the adoption of a family planning policy would evoke vehement

76

opposition within the Islamic leadership and in wide sectors of the population in Jordan, especially the lower socioeconomic strata in both rural areas and the large cities.

Two opposing factors acted to promote the adoption of a national family planning policy:

(1) In the early 1970s, and again from the mid-1980s onward, Jordan experienced economic difficulties as a result of large waves of immigration along with other factors, prompting Jordanian demographers and economists to advocate a reduction in the fertility rate of the population in order to sustain high economic growth rates.[30] This brought about the beginning of governmental involvement in the field of family planning in the early 1970s, namely, by allowing the Jordan Family Planning Association to operate in the East Bank. Similarly, the economic crises at the end of the 1980s and in the early 1990s spurred another leap forward, by permitting sterilization as well as contraceptive guidance in the villages. These developments ultimately led to the decision in 1993 to increase the level of governmental involvement in the area of family planning.

(2) From the 1960s onward, Western governments, especially the United States, as well as voluntary organizations in Europe and North America, attempted to persuade Third World countries with high rates of population increase to adopt national birth control policies and to allow activity by voluntary organizations in this field. Not all countries responded favorably to either of these requests, but Jordan, exposed to external pressures, had difficulty resisting the argument for a birth control policy, and in the 1960s voluntary activity was allowed to operate within the kingdom. Initially permitted in the West Bank only, this activity was readily extended to the East Bank after the economic crisis of the early 1970s. That the government initially permitted a voluntary organization to operate only in the West Bank hints at a differential approach on its part toward fertility, at least through 1967, i.e., encouraging birth control primarily in the Palestinian population of the West Bank.

Significantly, the contraceptive prevalence rate rose appreciably between the mid-1970s and the end of the 1980s — from 23 percent in 1967 to 35 percent in 1990, with the greatest increase occurring in the latter half of the 1980s.[31] This rise was characterized by the sharp increase in the relative proportion of women using IUDs (from 8.8 percent of total contraception users in 1976 to 43.7 percent in 1990). A more moderate rise, but of great significance,

77

was the rate of sterilization as a contraceptive method (from 8.3 percent in 1973 to 16 percent in 1990). In parallel, the relative proportion of women using the pill dropped sharply (from 52.2 percent of total contraception users in 1976 to only 3.1 percent in 1990).[32]

According to the 1990 survey, a relatively large number of couples using modern contraceptive methods (IUDs, sterilization and the pill) — 44.1 percent — acquired them through the private sector (private doctors, pharmacies and private hospitals). By contrast, the role played by government institutions in providing family planning services was relatively small. In particular, the contribution of the Maternal and Child Health Centers sponsored by the Ministry of Health provided services only to 6.1 percent of the total contraception users in 1990. However, governmental institutions, together with voluntary organizations supported by the government, supplied services to more than half the contraception users (54.4 percent in 1990).[33]

According to Jordanian demographers, an important factor in the rise in the contraceptive prevalence rate and the reduction in the total fertility rate was the government's family planning policy during the 1980s.[34] The services offered by voluntary organizations and the private sector also made a vital contribution to changes in the contraceptive prevalence rate. Moreover, social changes that took place in the kingdom from the 1970s onward also had a great influence. Two social developments in particular had an important influence on fertility levels: reduced rates of infant mortality, and the rise in educational level in Jordanian society, especially with regard to women — developments in which the government played a major part.

NOTES

1. See, WB, e.g., *World Tables, 1989–90 Edition*, Baltimore and London: Johns Hopkins University Press, 1990, pp. 332–33 (hereafter: *World Tables*).
2. *al-Ra'y* (Amman), 26 August 1992.
3. Ibid., 2 September 1992.
4. WB, *World Tables 1993*, pp. 354–55.
5. HKJ, *Jordan Population and Family Health Survey 1990*, Amman and Columbia (Maryland): DS and IRD/Macro International, 1992, pp. 23–24, tables 3.2 and 3.3 (hereafter: *JPFHS 1990*).
6. DS, *SY 1991*, p. 25, table 2/5.
7. Ibid. *1981*, p. 12, table 8.
8. *al-Ra'y* (Amman), 29 January 1990.

9. *Jordan Times*, 14 October 1991.
10. Ibid.
11. *al-Dunya*, 2 April 1992; *Jordan Times*, 2 November 1993.
12. *Jordan Times*, 2 November 1993.
13. Ibid., 7 August 1993. See also *International Herald Tribune*, 25 May 1993.
14. *Jordan Times*, 8 November 1992.
15. Ibid.
16. WB, *World Development Report 1990*, p. 206, table 15; *1991*, p. 233, table 15; *1992*, p. 246, table 15; *1993*, p. 266, table 15. See also *Jordan Times*, 28 and 29 May 1992.
17. See below p. 75.
18. UN, ESCWA, Social Development and Population Division, *Population Situation in the ESCWA Region 1990*, n.p. [Amman]: ESCWA, 1992, pp. 101–2 (hereafter: ESCWA, *Population Situation 1990*).
19. Charles W. Warren et al., "Fertility and Family Planning in Jordan: Results from the 1985 Jordan Husbands' Fertility Survey," *Studies in Family Planning* 21/1(1990): 33–34 (herafter: Warren).
20. ESCWA, *Population Situation 1990*, p. 101.
21. Hanna Rizk, "Trends in Fertility and Family Planning in Jordan," *Studies in Family Planning* 8/1 (1977): 91 (hereafter: Rizk).
22. Ibid.
23. Abdallah Abdel-Aziz et al., "Family Planning in Jordan: 1983 Survey Data," *Studies in Family Planning* 17/4 (1986): 202; Warren, p. 34.
24. *JPFHS 1990*, p. 47, table 4.11.
25. Ibid.
26. Abdel Rahim Omran, *Family Planning in the Legacy of Islam*, London and New York: Routledge, 1992, p. 255. See also Rizk, p. 91.
27. *Jordan Times*, 10 February 1993.
28. DS, *SY 1991*, p. 19, table 2/1.
29. Charles B. Keely and Bassam Saket, "Jordanian Migrant Workers in the Arab Region: A Case Study of Consequences for Labor Supplying Countries," *MEJ* 38/4 (1984): 694–96.
30. *Jordan Times*, 8 June 1992, 3 April, 5 May 1993.
31. *JPFHS 1990*, p. 39, table 4.5.
32. Ibid., p. 47, table 4.11.
33. Ibid.
34. Ibid., p. 37.

5

Nasser's Soft Revolution

INTRODUCTION

At different times between July 1952 and the late 1960s, the Egyptian government initiated various measures aimed at changing development trends in Egypt's society and economy. Three areas of focus, essentially interrelated, were population growth, domestic saving and economic growth. Other areas were also given attention, but there is no doubt that the first three were considered the prime areas in which far-reaching changes affecting the economy and the general welfare of the population could be achieved. The politics and performance of the Nasser regime in these areas have already been analyzed in a number of studies.[1] This chapter seeks to examine these changes from a long-term perspective, with the objective of contributing to an understanding of the nature of the July revolution of 1952.

In many ways, the 1850s and the early 1860s mark the beginning of a new period in the economic history of Egypt. It was at this time, for instance, that cotton first became the main agricultural commodity in terms of its contribution to GDP. Likewise, Egypt's integration in the world economy intensified: there was a marked increase of European involvement in the Egyptian economy (in digging the Suez Canal, laying railways, land reclamation, etc.), and Egyptian rulers started to become heavily indebted to European financial institutions. In some of those years the Egyptian economy showed impressive growth, and there was even a rise in living standards among a wide range of groups within the population. At this time, too, the saving patterns of the Egyptian elite took

80

form. In addition, it was during this period that the population growth began to be apparent. In short, these years marked the beginning of a period that was to last about a century and which, from many points of view, may be considered a time of laissez-faire in modern Egyptian history. It was brought to an end by the 1952 revolution.

Just as it is helpful to compare the changes of the Nasser period of the revolution with those of the four preceding generations, so is it helpful to review them against the background of developments that took place in the post-Nasser period. Accordingly, the following pages compare the changes in natural increase, patterns of domestic saving and economic growth in what may be seen as the first phase of the revolution in Egypt, the years of the Nasser regime, with those of the regimes that preceded and followed it.

NATURAL INCREASE

Little is known about birth and death rates in Egypt before the census of 1897, but it is generally agreed that crude estimates of birthrates during much of the closing decades of the nineteenth century stood at 40-45 per thousand.[2] With the introduction of the census, figures on the development of the birthrate became more firmly based. After a decline in the birthrate during the First World War, it stabilized in the 1920s at about 41-43 per thousand, and remained steady thereafter for about 45 years, until the mid-1960s. Only occasionally was the birthrate higher or lower than the figure noted: in 1942-43 and in 1957 it fell to 38-39 per thousand; and in 1936, 1950-52, and 1961 it rose to 44-45 per thousand. In 1967, however, it began to fall, a trend that continued until 1971 when it stabilized at 36 per thousand. This rate was maintained throughout the first half of the 1970s, producing a birthrate 15-16 percent lower than in most of the 1950s and the first half of the 1960s. Contrary to most demographic forecasts made at the start of the 1970s, however, in the second half of the 1970s and the beginning of the 1980s the birthrate not only ceased falling, it even rose slightly, stabilizing in the years 1975-84 at around 37 per thousand.[3]

The trend in the death rate was more uniform, falling from an estimated 35 per thousand at the end of the nineteenth century[4] to 26-28 per thousand by the beginning of the 1920s. This rate was sustained for about 25 years, until the middle of the 1940s. Since the Second World War there has been a continuous decline.

81

In 1948–51 the death rate fell to 19–20 per thousand; by the end of the 1950s it was 15–16 per thousand; and some 20 years later, at the end of the 1970s, it stabilized at around 10 per thousand. In 1984 and 1985 still lower death rates were registered — around 9 per thousand. Hence, in the course of the present century (until the mid-1980s) the death rate has fallen by about 74 percent. From the end of the Second World War to the mid-1980s alone it decreased by about 67 percent. Clearly, this was a very steep decline.[5]

It is the difference in the pace of decline of death rates and birthrates, especially since the 1920s, that explains both the rise in the rate of natural increase and the length of time over which this increase has been maintained. From rates of natural increase which fluctuated between 7 and 10 per thousand in the latter decades of the nineteenth century, they rose to 15–16 per thousand in the 1930s and in the years immediately following the Second World War. During most of the 1950s and 1960s there was a further significant rise, to around 26 per thousand. Then for five consecutive years, from 1968 to 1972, a decline occurred: average natural increase during these years was 21.3 per thousand. This was followed by a remarkable shift: not only did natural increase rates rise yet again, they attained levels never previously reached. In 1979 and 1985, peak rates of 29.2 and 30.4, respectively, were registered, and the average rate of natural increase in the decade from 1976 to 1985 reached 27.4.[6]

The meaning of these high rates in absolute terms is well known. At the end of the nineteenth century the population numbered 10 million, and it took about fifty years for the increase of a further 10 million. From the base of 20 million in 1949, 17 years were required for the next 10 million (30 million in 1966), then 12 years to reach 40 million in 1978, and eight years only to reach 50 million in 1988.[7] The effect of this enormous increase in Egypt's population in recent generations has already been studied. Here it will suffice to mention that the country's other resources increased in this period at lower aggregate rates, a circumstance that first led to "accumulating difficulties"[8] and then to the growing impoverishment of the economy.[9] The only Middle Eastern country in the 1960s and 1970s whose GNP per capita was lower than that of Egypt was Sudan. All the other countries of the region, including such non-oil economies as the Arab Republic of Yemen, Morocco, Jordan and Syria, attained higher figures.[10]

The birthrate trend in the 1960s and early 1970s requires some explanation, particularly the decline in the five years from 1968 to 1972. Scholars are divided over the causes and meaning of this decline, which some see as a result of the new population policy adopted by the Egyptian government following the revolution.[11] Whereas the monarchy had favored rapid population growth — whether out of economic considerations (falling wages and rising land rents) or out of a traditional world view[12] — the Nasser regime adopted a different approach. It viewed high population growth rates as a major obstacle to the rapid development of the economy and to a fundamental change in its structure. Consequently, the government, wanting to bring about a decline in birthrates, favored a national policy of birth control.[13]

The implementation of this policy was marked by two characteristics. First, public declarations of policy notwithstanding, there was a lengthy delay in its operational formulation and activation. Statements concerning the need for family planning and the establishment of birth control clinics were made by Egypt's leaders as early as 1954. In May 1962 Nasser stated at the Congress of Popular Forces that population growth was one of the most serious hindrances to the economic development of Egypt, and that there was no alternative to the adoption of birth control by modern methods.[14] However, by mid-1965, 13 years after the seizure of power, comprehensive and effective measures to achieve this had yet to be taken. There were still only 28 family planning clinics in the whole country, most of them in the major cities, and only some of them were operating regularly.[15] Only in 1966 did the government undertake wide-ranging measures. In February, a Higher Council for Family Planning, headed by Prime Minister Zakariyya Muhi al-Din, began functioning, and in August it was announced that 2,850 family planning clinics were operating throughout the country.[16]

The second characteristic of the family planning program was the limited scope of its operations, manifested in three areas: duration, coverage and geographical extent. The limited duration of consistent operation and funding was perhaps the most important factor. Thus, although the program had actually taken off only in 1966, by 1973 the intensity of implementation appeared to have lessened.[17] It was surely no coincidence that the subject of rapid population growth and the need to continue with family planning did not appear in the October Paper (April 1974), in which Sadat presented his concepts and policies. The omission was particularly glaring because most of the document dealt with Egypt's internal problems.[18] The reduction in the scope of operations continued throughout the second half of the 1970s, so that by the first half of the 1980s it was difficult to point to any measures of significance being undertaken in this area. During this period the authorities concentrated on efforts to change behavior patterns through simple messages such as *"usra saghira — hayat afdal"* ("small family — better life") in the media, and other forms of mass advertising.[19] Some critics claim that the direct family planning policy was actually abandoned in 1972/73,[20] meaning that the direct antinatalist policy lasted for only seven years (from 1966 to 1972).

Even in those years, the number of women taking part in family planning programs was very small. In September 1972 official figures stated that of some 7 million women of childbearing age (15–44), only 706,000 were prepared to use contraceptives.[21] Similarly, the number of women who had ever visited family planning clinics was reported to be extremely low. In the Cairo district, for example, only 9 percent, and in the Minufiyya district only 7.5 percent, of all women of childbearing age had visited such clinics in 1971.[22]

Implementation was also restricted from a geographical and social viewpoint. The more active clinics were mostly those in the big cities, where in any case more women were exposed to influences that could bring about a voluntary reduction in the fertility rate, and had access as well to contraceptives other than through the family planning clinics. In rural areas, the effectiveness of the clinics was highly circumscribed.[23]

The apparent correlation between the years of decline in birthrates and the years of more intensive activity to encourage family planning — the late 1960s and early 1970s — might be taken as an indication of a causal connection. However, the existence of such causality should not be taken for granted. First, in at least two cases in the preceding generation there was a similar significant decline without the existence of a birth control campaign. Between 1941 and 1944 birthrates fell to between 37.6 and 40.4 per thousand, and in 1955–57 to between 38.0 and 40.7 per thousand. In both cases the decline was from birthrates of 43–45 per thousand.[24] The accepted explanation for the decline in the 1940s was the severe economic conditions in Egypt as a result of the Second World War.[25] There is no such easy explanation for the decline in the 1950s, for the decline was already well established before the 1956 war. However, it is clear that the fall in the birthrate in both cases was not the outcome of deliberate measures undertaken by the government. If a decline in the birthrate was possible in Egypt in the 1940s and 1950s without government intervention, then the fall at the end of the 1960s might also have been the consequence of factors other than official measures. It has been suggested that it is more likely that the decline was primarily the result of the deep crisis in which Egypt was caught up during the period between the 1967 and 1973 wars.[26] In other words, this was a similar development to that which had occurred during the Second World War.

Whatever the reason for the fall in the birthrate between 1968 and 1972 (most likely a combination of both factors), one thing is clear: Nasser's regime did not generate sufficiently strong social and economic forces for an effective family planning policy to take root. Possibly, the revolutionaries did not really believe in the effectiveness of family planning as the panacea for Egypt's ills. Moreover, it seems that although the leaders of the revolution did indeed seek to bring about profound change, particularly after the severity of the population explosion and the inadequacy of alternative measures (such as facilitating emigration) had become evident, they did not have the necessary power to accomplish a comprehensive and radical shift in such a sensitive area.

One of the main constraining factors was the opposition of several religious groups to state interference in the natural order. This opposition was in some cases forceful and vociferous, in others more restrained.[27] Two aspects of this opposition are particularly relevant. First, most of the clerics on the lower levels, those in daily contact with the rural population and city dwellers of the lower social strata, rejected the economic justification for the use of contraceptives.[28] Second, Nasser, and still more Sadat, sensed that open confrontation with the clerics could have severe consequences for the stability of their rule. In this context, it may be remembered that the most bitter experience in the struggle to secure the revolution in the 1950s had been with the Muslim Brethren.[29]

At the beginning of his rule Sadat had wanted to create a new modus vivendi with the Brethren.[30] However, it would seem to have been no coincidence that shortly after giving the Brethren permission to openly engage in their activities in 1971, Sadat's government began to restrict its operations in the field of family planning, while giving considerable publicity to Western studies showing that a rise in income and living standards was accompanied by a decline in women's fertility.[31] With the Egyptian economy achieving a high level of economic growth from 1974, accompanied by a rise in consumption rates, it appeared feasible to leave the problem of high birthrates to the free play of economic and social factors. This approach not only prevented confrontation with the clerics and the masses under their influence, but also gave Sadat an additional justification for seeking Western aid, on the grounds that such aid would make a vital contribution to reducing Egypt's population growth.[32] The population, however, did not respond to rising living standards as envisaged: despite a considerable real per capita rise in consumption between 1974 and 1984 even among the lowest deciles of the population,[33] birthrates did not fall.

Although the forces the Egyptian leaders were attempting to oppose were extremely powerful and long-lived, the fact remains that the efforts to stem the population explosion in Egypt until the mid-1980s were tardy, short-lived and inadequate. The attempt to break this cycle toward the end of Nasser's rule failed. Following Gunnar Myrdal, who asserted that there was a firm link between poverty and "soft government,"[34] John Kenneth Galbraith has suggested that there is a connection between "soft government" and the failure to arrest a population explosion.[35] Is there, in fact, such a vicious circle? Does poverty always lead to a "soft state," lacking any real chance of contending with an ever-increasing population, so that poverty reproduces itself? Not necessarily — Galbraith himself cited demographic developments in China and in the Punjab region of India in the 1960s and 1970s to prove it.[36] True, doubts have been raised as to the extent of the success both in China and in the Punjab,[37] but there have been other cases, not less impressive. Egypt in the late 1980s is one of them.[38]

DOMESTIC SAVING

Since Isma'il's time until the 1980s, with the exception of only a few years, the Egyptian economy has been characterized by low rates of domestic saving.[39] More precisely, throughout this lengthy period the rate of increase in real capital assets from domestic sources has been low. There are two major reasons for this for the years before the revolution: the export of the profits of foreign companies to their shareholders abroad, and the widening gap in the distribution of capital and income in Egyptian society. The low rate of domestic saving is deemed one of the main factors responsible for the "accumulating difficulties" of the period between the First World War and the 1952 revolution, particularly owing to the low rate of local private sector investment in agriculture and industry. Throughout the entire period the government took no real steps to encourage higher rates of saving among the middle and upper classes.[40]

In this area too the Nasser regime sought to initiate change. The agrarian reform was supposed to bring about, among other things, a rise in domestic saving, which was to come about as a result of increased savings on the part of the fellahin who had recently become smallholders.[41] The nationalization of foreign-owned companies was likewise expected to cause an increase in domestic saving, as profits would no longer be remitted to shareholders abroad. In the event, however, there was hardly any change: for most of the years of the Nasser regime, domestic savings stood at about 12 percent of GNP. The significance of this is that most, if not all, of the increase in real capital assets in this period came through capital import, that is, from foreign loans and grants,[42] and once there was a sharp drop in capital import it was no longer possible to maintain high investment rates.

In the last three years of the Nasser regime, the domestic saving rate, already relatively low, fell steeply. This was the result of a sharp fall in government saving following the increasing current expenditure on defense after the 1967 war, the rising cost of maintaining a swelling public administration, and the beginning of a policy of substantial subsidies on essential commodities.[43] Thus, the revolution not only failed to bring about an increase in the domestic saving rate, it provided the causes for its further decline. Far from instituting compulsory saving, the revolution actually facilitated a rise in aggregate consumption.

The rate of domestic saving continued to fall in the 1970s to a low point similar to that of the years immediately after the Second World War. Many factors contributed to this process, but the main ones were the rise, in real terms, in government expenditure on subsidies for essential commodities and the continuing expansion of public sector employment.[44]

ECONOMIC GROWTH

Egypt enjoyed specific periods of growth in real GDP between the 1860s and the 1980s. Besides the great booms that opened and closed this period — the cotton boom and the oil boom — there were three other periods of high growth, making a total of five such waves in the course of over 125 years: 1861–65, 1903–7, 1948–52, 1960–65 and 1974–85.[45] Analysis shows that high growth was attained when one of two factors (or both) was present: a rapid rise in levels of income from the export of raw materials, and a rise in the import of capital due to increased external borrowing, unilateral transfers and investment by foreign nationals and companies.

The connection between growth and high income from the export of raw materials is present in four of the five periods of growth. In the first three, massive revenue was generated by cotton exports, in the fifth, through the export of crude oil. Only after the revolution was there a period of growth fired by the import of capital rather than by the export of raw materials. In all four cases, the growth of income from exports arose from the combination of a sharp rise in the price of raw materials on the world market and an increase in the quantities exported. The increase in income that was generated by the massive export of cotton contributed greatly to the development of the Egyptian economy, prompting investment in agriculture, transport and finances, and an increase in the living standard of major sections of the population. However, growth predicated solely on the export of raw materials created an undesirable economic dynamic. This was due to the almost total dependence of the economy on external developments over which it had either no control at all, or very restricted control at best. In other words, economic growth was entirely, or almost entirely, beyond the control of the Egyptian economy. Thus, the growth periods of the economy before the revolution were due, in general terms, to the American Civil War and the Korean War, and after the revolution to the consequences of the Iran-Iraq War.

From certain points of view, the revolution sought to break this relationship. Nasser perceived that the Egyptian economy had to undergo the fundamental structural change of turning industry into the leading sector. However, when the time came to put this perception into practice, in the framework of the first Five-Year Plan (1960–65), the regime found itself in a situation similar to that which had marked earlier periods in its economic history: a period of growth associated with the massive import of capital, principally in the form of loans and unilateral transfers from abroad, from both the public and private sectors. Such a relationship had been evident in the 1860s: parallel with the increase of revenues associated with the "cotton famine," Egyptian rulers — first Sa'id, then Isma'il — started borrowing on the European money market in amounts that fluctuated at first between £E 3 million and £E 7 million but soon reached far higher figures, until the total external debt came to £E 68.5 million.[46] This sum was 9.4 times higher than the total revenues of the Egyptian treasury in 1876, the year when Isma'il declared the state treasury bankrupt.[47] For many years thereafter Egypt was prevented, for all intents and purposes, from soliciting loans from abroad. As long as British officials determined the economic policy and development of Egypt, and as long as the bitter economic and political memory of the first external debt was retained by the local elite, Egypt was not a borrowing but a debt-paying state.

However, no sooner had Egypt attained its independence in the full sense of the word (that is, both economically and politically), than its leaders hurried to gather capital from abroad. Unlike Sa'id and Isma'il, Nasser did not have the good fortune to rule at a time of high income from the export of raw materials. His desire to change the structure of the economy and his refusal or inability to impose high rates of domestic saving on either the public or the private sectors left him no choice but to try to solicit resources elsewhere. He borrowed as much as he could and succeeded in obtaining sizable grants from foreign governments (principally the United States and the Soviet Union).[48]

The capital that Nasser mobilized, and the advanced technology that came with it, resulted in several structural and other changes whose impact on the Egyptian economy was to be felt for a long time afterward. According to one calculation, total gross investment in the Egyptian economy from 1952 to 1967 was equal to the total import of capital (loans and grants) during the same period. The Aswan High Dam, power stations, rural electrification and the establishment of heavy industry — all these and more were financed by imported capital. In contrast to the period of khedival splendor, the process of sinking into debt in the 1960s did not end in the bankruptcy of the Egyptian treasury; but even so, it was accompanied by an extremely grave crisis. By 1965 Nasser had exhausted his political and economic ability to obtain further loans for economic development. The burden of debt had grown so heavy that international banks and credit institutions were no longer prepared to provide loans in sums adequate for further investment.[49] Hence, the second Five-Year Plan (1966–70), intended to complete the first, never took off. One of the most important areas of activity of the post-revolutionary regime was interrupted for almost a decade, and when it was resumed in 1974, it was under different economic and political conditions. The cessation of the plan had a bearing on Egypt's foreign policy, and it contributed to the escalation that led to the 1967 war.

Nasser failed in his attempt to break the strong link between exogenous developments and the patterns of growth of the Egyptian economy. Moreover, his comprehensive efforts in this area paradoxically left behind an economy whose processes of growth were more firmly attached to, and more dependent on, external developments and capital import than ever before. The result was the reverse of what had been intended. This became evident in the two decades after Nasser's development policy had ground to a halt. He had planned to set up industries on such a scale as to effect a real change in the structure of the economy. Not only was this target missed, but the economic system that developed was self-defeating in that its mode of functioning obstructed future attempts at change. By imposing state control over a large part of the means of production, discouraging initiative on the part of the domestic private sector and driving foreign investors away, Nasser converted the public sector into Egypt's largest industrial entrepreneur. He did succeed in advancing the establishment of new industries in several fields, but at the price of stifling the influence of market forces and mechanisms and subjecting the entire sector to restrictive bureaucratic control. The nationalized industries soon became inefficient, unable to adapt to rapidly changing economic conditions, and above all wasteful of economic resources as well as foci of disguised unemployment and decreasing productivity.[50]

Among the many factors that defeated Nasser's attempts to bring about structural change in the Egyptian economy, the fact that his was a "soft" revolution loomed large. Its two primary manifestations were the establishment of top-heavy, sluggish economic bureaucracies, many of which were managed by inexperienced army officers; and the commitment given to students at the beginning of the 1960s, following rising tension on the campuses, to employ every university graduate who wished to work in the public sector. The result was that by the second half of the 1960s, the rate of annual increase in employment in the public sector was double that in the other sectors of the economy (3 percent versus 1.5 percent).[51] Moreover, this occurred when the rate of investment was at its lowest level since July 1952. The public sector in effect turned into a depository for surplus work force. These two developments, particularly the second, were a further reflection of the regime's unwillingness or inability to come to grips with pockets of resistance, preferring instead to soften opposition through material and other concessions whose eventual social and economic costs were very high.

No period like the dozen years from 1974 to 1985 in which the Egyptian economy achieved high economic growth — unequaled in rates and duration by anything it had previously attained during this century — better demonstrates the power of continuity. The prominent patterns that stood out during the four periods of growth since the 1860s recurred in the years of *infitah*. On the one hand, GDP grew on account of the swell of income through oil exports (and alternative income through the supply of domestic demand); on the other, there was a significant increase in imports during these years as a result of investment by foreign firms, and grants and loans to the government, as well as an additional element that had not existed in the past — remittances by Egyptian workers employed in the Arab oil states.[52] However, the rate of growth in agriculture and in industry lagged behind that of the GNP as a whole. Not only did industry fail to trigger economic growth in the post-Nasser period, it did not even undergo any marked change despite the great influx of resources into the country.[53] As in the past, high growth rates achieved in these years were all the result of exogenous developments; and as in the past, they did not bring about any fundamental structural change in the economy. The attempt, albeit limited, to achieve structural change was greatly impeded by the Nasserist etatist legacy.

It is also striking that, as in the first period of growth in the 1860s, but with even greater intensity, the years of growth at the end of the 1970s and in the 1980s were characterized by increasing foreign debt, swelling to $32 billion by 1984.[54] Once again the Egyptian economy had become weighed down by the burden of debt. The sums that Egypt began to transfer abroad in the mid-1980s for debt repayment amounted to $3 billion annually,[55] more than the country's total commercial exports excluding oil, and exceeding in value the total annual aid (civil and military) received from the United States. Most significantly, like previous booms, that of the 1980s did not create forces that would be able to maintain the level of growth when the influx of revenues and capital from external sources deteriorated.

91

CONCLUSION

The 1952 revolution came at the height of demographic and economic developments that had been in progress for several generations: high natural increase rates, low domestic saving rates, and fitful economic growth dependent on occurrences exogenous to the economy and on the import of capital. The revolution, which in many respects was the indirect offspring of these developments, eventually resolved to halt these processes. The Nasser regime indeed tried to change the course of demographic and economic developments, but the measures taken did not, in the final analysis, succeed in breaking the forces of continuity. In fact, the 1970s and the 1980s even witnessed the strengthening of trends that had existed between the two world wars and perhaps before.

The effort failed, possibly because it lacked determination and resolution, and also because the revolutionary regime drew back from the possible political price the changes might exact. Basically, the revolution lacked the kind of coherent ideology that could provide a solid conceptual base for the changes the regime wished to effect. Attempts to elaborate and develop such an ideology met with only partial success, as did efforts to win broad support from the masses via simplistic slogans. Furthermore, from its inception the revolution lacked the social basis which could provide the forces necessary to attain its goals. Its social basis was very narrow (the military and the bureau-technocracy), and by its very nature was incapable of recruiting the masses in the service of reform. Nasser was aware of this weakness and strove to broaden the base for social revolution, but to no avail.[56] This failure perhaps lies at the heart of the entire matter. The absence of broad support for the revolution obliged the regime to "buy" such support: subsidized commodities for the urban masses, guaranteed employment for university graduates, ever-growing allocations of resources to the army, and the like. It is on account of this need to gain the support of the masses and other social groups through granting material benefits — even at the price of perpetuating processes disastrous for the economy and society — that the 1952 revolution may be termed a "soft revolution."

Why did Nasser not gain the active support or active participation of the masses? Several feasible explanations have been suggested.[57] We may refer to the analysis by George Lefebvre, the historian of the French Revolution, concerning the conditions preceding that event. Lefebvre inductively reached the conclusion that what he called a "revolutionary crowd" — one that follows the revolutionary leadership in its drive for radical social change — will not exist unless an "appropriate collective mentality" has been created prior to the revolutionary events (namely, "the outbreak of the revolution").[58] By "appropriate collective mentality" Lefebvre means a new system of concepts, attitudes and images to which the crowd clings. Such a new normative system has enormous power and constitutes one of the elements that imparts to the masses their revolutionary qualities: the drive, sometimes the frenzy, to tear down the existing social, economic and political order and the willingness, sometimes the demand, to set up a new political and social order.

Egypt at the end of the 1940s and beginning of the 1950s was indeed in the throes of a profound social and political crisis. However, the change in the collective mentality — if such existed at all — was most limited in extent and power. This assessment is based, among other things, on the fact that following the seizure of power in Egypt in 1952 by the Free Officers there was no broadly based popular movement, either organized or spontaneous, that joined in the protest, far less the struggle, against the existing political, social and economic order. There were attempts, to be sure, by the Muslim Brethren on the one hand and the Communist Party and the workers' unions on the other to activate the masses, particularly in the large cities, but these were largely devoid of any manifestations of change in the collective mentality. This was even more pronounced in the villages: expressions of pent-up anger, however long harbored by the peasants against their masters, were rare in the revolution of 1952. The combination in Egypt of a revolutionary political elite lacking a crystallized conceptualization of the desired political, social and economic order, and urban and rural masses who underwent no radical change of attitude regarding the existing order, could produce no more than a "soft revolution."

NOTES

1. See Charles Issawi, *Egypt in Revolution: An Economic Analysis*, London: Oxford University Press, 1963 (hereafter: Issawi, *Revolution*); Bent Hansen and Girgis A. Marzouk, *Development and Economic Policy in the UAR (Egypt)*, Amsterdam: North-Holland Publishing Co., 1965 (hereafter: Hansen and Marzouk); Donald C. Mead, *Growth and Structural Change in the Egyptian Economy*, Homewood, Ill.: Richard D. Irwin, 1967 (hereafter: Mead); Rashed Al-Barawy, *Economic Development*

in the United Arab Republic (Egypt), Cairo: The Anglo-Egyptian Bookshop, 1972; Robert Mabro, *The Egyptian Economy 1952-1972*, Oxford: Clarendon Press, 1974 (hereafter: Mabro); Mahmoud Abdel-Fadel, *The Political Economy of Nasserism*, Cambridge: Cambridge University Press, 1980; John Waterbury, *Egypt: Burdens of the Past, Options for the Future*, Bloomington: Indiana University Press, 1978 (hereafter: Waterbury, *Burdens*); id., *The Egypt of Nasser and Sadat*, Princeton: Princeton University Press, 1983 (hereafter: Waterburg, *Nasser and Sadat*).

2. Justin McCarthy, "Nineteenth-Century Egyptian Population," *MES* 12 (1976): 21-25 (hereafter: McCarthy); cf. Daniel Panzac, "The Population of Egypt in the Nineteenth Century," *AAS* 21 (1987): 22 (hereafter: Panzac).

3. For complete data series, see CAPMAS, *The Increase of Population in the United Arab Republic*, Cairo, 1969 (hereafter: CAPMAS, *Increase of Population*); id., *SY 1952-1971*; id., *SY 1952-1985*; Mead, p. 302; Mabro, p. 29.

4. McCarthy, ibid.; cf. Panzac, ibid.

5. See sources in n. 3.

6. Ibid.

7. Mead, p. 302; CAPMAS, *SY 1952-1985*, pp. 6-8.

8. Issawi, *Revolution*, pp. 32-45.

9. See, e.g., A.B. Mountjoy, "Egypt: Population and Resources," in J.I. Clarke and W.B. Fisher (eds.), *Populations of the Middle East and North Africa*, London: University of London Press, 1972, pp. 303-12; Waterbury, *Burdens*, pp. 85-124.

10. WB, *World Development Report 1980*, pp. 110-11, table 1.

11. Abdel-Rahim Omran, *Population in the Arab World*, New York: UNFPA, 1980, p. 89.

12. Gabriel Baer, *'Arviye ha-mizrah ha-tikhon*, 2nd ed., Tel Aviv: Hakibbutz Hameuchad, 1973, p. 39 (hereafter: Baer), quoting Muhammad 'Ali 'Alluba, *Mabadi' fi'l siyasa al-misriyya*, Cairo, 1942; and Hafiz 'Afifi, *'Ala hamish al-siyasa*, Cairo, 1948.

13. See further Azriel Karni, "Temurot be-yahas la-piquah 'al ha-yeluda ba-mizrah ha-tikhon," *Hamizrah Hehadash* 17 (1967): 231-33 (hereafter: Karni).

14. Ibid., p. 232.

15. Ibid., pp. 233-34.

16. *al-Ahram*, 6 August 1966.

17. Khalid Ikram, *Egypt: Economic Management in a Period of Transition*, Baltimore: Johns Hopkins University Press, 1980, p. 111 (hereafter: Ikram).

18. For an analysis of the October Paper, see Shimon Shamir, *Mitzrayim be-hanhagat Sadat*, Tel Aviv: Dvir, 1978, pp. 117-39.

19. Centre d'Etudes et de Documentation Economiques, Juridiques et Socialies, *La Campagne de controle des naissances en Egypte 1980-1981*, Cairo, 1982, vol. 2, pp. 29-35, 39-42.

20. D. MacKenzie of the *New Scientist* reported from Cairo in October 1985 that "experts in Cairo blame the head of the National Family Planning Commission for the last 11 years, Aziz Bindari. Bindari supports the view, espoused by the UN Population Conference in Bucharest in 1972, that, because populations have leveled off in the rich world, economic development is itself the best 'pill'. Supporters of this view regard attempts to introduce birth control alone to poor societies as coercive. Under Bindari's control, funds for family planning in Egypt were allocated 'to sewing machines and scientific conferences'.... It's not that Bindari was against family planning...it's just that no one did anything about it. It was supposed to just follow naturally the economic development.... Bindari took precious family-planning funds and spent them on development as well." "Tackling Egypt's Baby Boom," *The Middle East* (Oct. 1985): 51.

21. *al-Ahram*, 24 September 1972.

22. Ibid., 22 March 1972.

23. Ikram, p. 111.

24. CAPMAS, *Increase of Population*.

94

25. On the economic conditions during the war years, see Robert L. Tignor, *State, Private Enterprise, and Economic Change in Egypt, 1918-1952*, Princeton: Princeton University Press, 1984, 215-16.
26. Ikram, pp. 108-9; Waterbury, *Nasser and Sadat*, p. 45.
27. For examples of the various attitudes of Egyptian clerics to family planning, see Karni, 238-39; Baer, pp. 42-43; *al-Sha'b*, 2 August 1979; *al-Ahram*, 8 February 1981; *al-Nur*, 8 December 1982, 3 August 1983.
28. Karni, p. 239.
29. See also Richard P. Mitchell, *The Society of the Muslim Brothers*, London: Oxford University Press, 1969, pp. 125-51.
30. O. Carré and G. Michaud, *Les Frères Musulmans: Egypte et Syrie, 1928-1982*, Paris, 1983, pp. 67-70.
31. R. Anker and G. Farook, "Population and Socio-Economic Development: The New Perspective," *International Labor Review* 17 (1978): 143-55; UN, Department of International Economic and Social Affairs, *Demographic Transition and Socio-Economic Development*, New York: UN, 1979.
32. At the same time, however, Egypt's foreign creditors expected "serious steps" to be taken by the government to curb population increase. See Waterbury, *Nasser and Sadat*, pp. 45-46.
33. See e.g., Unni Wikan, "Living Conditions among Cairo's Poor: A View from Below," *MEJ* 39 (1985): 7-26.
34. Myrdal writes: "When we characterize...countries as 'soft states' we mean that...national governments require extraordinarily little of their citizens. There are few obligations either to do things in the interest of the community or to avoid actions opposed to that interest. Even those obligations that do exist are enforced inadequately if at all...*there is little hope in South Asia for rapid development without greater social discipline*...in the absence of more discipline — which will not appear without regulations backed by compulsion — all measures for rural uplift will be largely ineffective." *Asian Drama: An Inquiry into the Poverty of Nations*, New York: Twentieth Century Fund, 1968, vol. 2, pp. 895-96 (emphasis added).
35. John K. Galbraith, *The Age of Uncertainty*, Boston: 1977, pp. 285, 287.
36. Ibid., p. 287.
37. E.J. Croll, "The Single-Child Family: The First Five Years," in Neville Maxwell and Bruce McFarlane (eds.), *China's Changed Road to Development*, Oxford: Pergamon Press, 1984, p. 133.
38. See further below, pp. 113-17, 120-27.
39. Bent Hansen, "Savings and Investments, Flow of Funds: Egypt 1884-1914," Working Paper No. 135, Department of Economics, University of California, Berkeley (1979); id., "Savings in the UAR (Egypt), 1938/39 and 1945/46 to 1962/63," Institute of National Planning, Memo. 551 (Cairo, 1965) (hereafter: Hansen, "Savings in the UAR"); Issawi, *Revolution*, p. 124; Mead, pp. 216-17, tables 9.1, 9.2; Hansen and Marzouk, pp. 224-29, 324-25; Ikram, pp. 396-97, table 5.
40. See, e.g., Charles Issawi, *Egypt at Mid-Century: An Economic Survey*, London: Oxford University Press, 1954, pp. 89-90; Hansen, "Savings in the UAR."
41. Gabriel S. Saab, *The Egyptian Agrarian Reform 1952-1962*, London: Oxford University Press, 1967, pp. 21ff.
42. Mead, p. 220; Ikram, p. 44.
43. Ikram, pp. 54-55.
44. Ikram, pp. 328-29; Nazih N.M. Ayubi, "Bureaucratic Inflation and Administrative Inefficiency: The Deadlock in Egyptian Administration," *MES* 18 (1982): 288-89.
45. For data and analysis, see Bent Hansen, "Preliminary Report on an Attempt to Estimate National Product and Income for Egypt, c. 1880-1913," Institute of International Studies, University of California (Berkeley), 1974); id., "Income and Consumption in Egypt, 1886/1887 to 1937," *IJMES* 10 (1979): 27-47; Mead, pp. 44-45, tables 3.1, 3.2, and pp. 286-89, IA. 6, IA. 7; Ikram, pp. 398-99, table 5;

Hansen and Marzouk, 2–7, pp. 318–20; CAPMAS, *SY 1952–1985*, p. 253; WB, *World Development Report 1986*, p. 192, table 2.

46. Abdel Maqsud Hamza, *The Public Debt of Egypt, 1854–1876*, Cairo, 1944, pp. 256–57.
47. For figures on the Egyptian treasury, see A.E. Crouchley, *The Economic Development of Modern Egypt*, London: Longmans, 1938, pp. 274–76.
48. For data on loans and grants received, see Ikram, pp. 343–44; Nazem Abdalla, "The Role of Foreign Capital in Egypt's Economic Development: 1960–1972," *IJMES* 14 (1982): 87–92.
49. Ikram, p. 357; Bent Hansen and Karim Nashashibi, *Foreign Trade Regimes and Economic Development: Egypt*, New York: Columbia University Press, 1975, pp. 108, 111.
50. Eliyahu Kanovsky, *The Economic Impact of the Six-Day War*, New York: Praeger Publishers, 1970, pp. 230–31, 251, 255 (hereafter: Kanovsky); Ikram, pp. 255–56.
51. Ikram, p. 38.
52. CAPMAS, *SY 1952–1985*, p. 273; Institute for Financial Studies, *International Financial Statistics* (July 1986), pp. 192–95; WB, *World Development Report 1986*, p. 206, table 14.
53. WB, *World Development Report 1986*, p. 182, table 2.
54. Ibid., p. 208, table 15.
55. Ibid., pp. 210, 212, tables 16, 17.
56. Shimon Shamir, "Shqi'at ha-meshihiyut ha-naseristit," in id. (ed.), *Yeridat ha-nasserizm, 1965–1970*, Tel Aviv: Mif'alim Universitayyim, 1978, pp. 21–24, 37–38; P.J. Vatikiotis, *Nasser and His Generation*, London: Croom Helm, 1978.
57. Richard H. Dekmejian, *Egypt under Nasir*, Albany: SUNY Press, 1971, pp. 54–55, 153–54; Waterbury, *Nasser and Sadat*, pp. 311–15, 332.
58. Georges Lefebvre, "Revolutionary Crowds," in Jeffry Kaplow (ed.), *New Perspectives on the French Revolution*, New York: John Wiley, 1965, p. 180.

6

Population Pressure and Oil Revenues:
Egypt and Saudi Arabia, 1962–85

INTRODUCTION

A complex and changeable relationship developed between the two major Arab countries on either side of the Red Sea basin, Egypt and Saudi Arabia, from the beginning of the 1960s until the mid-1980s, one which was to have an important influence on Egypt's regional policies in the economic area and ultimately on developments in the Middle East as a whole.

The two states differed greatly in many respects; in fact, in three important socioeconomic areas their circumstances were almost totally polarized. First, Egypt had a large population, both in absolute and relative terms (total population in proportion to GNP), which had been increasing at high rates since the 1950s — approximately 2.5 percent annually — for most of the period. Conversely, the population of Saudi Arabia was small, both absolutely and relatively, despite an increase at high rates in the last generation (see table 6.1).

Second, the Egyptian economy grew at extremely low rates throughout most of the period between the First World War and 1973. This, together with high natural increase rates, resulted in a gradual deterioration of the standard of living. At the beginning of the 1970s, the average per capita income in real terms was lower than that estimated for the start of the century. Although there was a considerable rise in the growth rates of the economy between 1974 and 1985, Egypt in the mid-1980s belonged to the group of countries in which the annual per capita GNP stood at $550–750.

Table 6.1

Egypt and Saudi Arabia: economic and social indicators,
1978 and 1984

	Egypt	Saudi Arabia
Population (in millions)		
1978	39.9	8.2[a]
1984	45.9	11.1[a]
Natural increase rate (per thousand)		
1978	24	36
1984	26	34
GNP per capita (US$, current prices)		
1978	660	7,690
1984	720	10,530
Energy consumption per capita[b]		
1978	463	1,306
1984	562	3,602
Merchandise trade (millions of US$)		
1978 Exports	1,901	40,716
Imports	6,480	20,424
1984 Exports	5,286	46,845
Imports	14,596	33,696
Current account balance (millions of US$)		
1978	-540	+12,793
1984	-1,978	-24,036

Notes:
a   Including foreign nationals.
b   Kilogram of oil equivalent.

Sources:
WB, *World Development Report 1980*, pp. 110–11, 122–25, 134–35, 144–45, tables 1, 7, 8, 13, 18; *1986*, pp. 180–81, 194–97, 206–7, 230–31. tables 1, 8, 9, 14, 26.

By contrast, the resources at the disposal of the Saudi economy rose sharply in the 1960s and 1970s. A particularly steep rise in revenues was recorded during 1973–82, the years of the "oil decade." This was due to both the dramatic rise in oil prices and the increase in the quantity of oil exported. In terms of annual GNP per capita, Saudi Arabia in 1984 belonged in the same category as such countries as Japan and West Germany (see table 6.2).

The third area of divergence between the two societies is that Egypt began to experience modernization in many spheres from the start of the nineteenth century, much before Saudi Arabia. One manifestation of this process in Egypt was the development of its educational system, including secondary and higher education. In the last generation a major increase has been recorded in the number of secondary school and university students, reaching

Table 6.2

Economic indicators of selected low-income and high-income economies, 1984

	Population mid-1984 (millions)	GNP per capita 1984 (US$)	Average annual growth rate 1965–84 (percent)
Indonesia	158.9	540	4.9
Yemen Arab Republic	7.8	550	5.9
Cote d'Ivoire	9.9	610	0.2
Philippines	53.4	660	2.6
Morocco	21.4	670	2.8
Egypt	45.9	720	4.3
Nigeria	96.5	730	2.8
United Kingdom	56.4	8,570	1.6
France	54.9	9,760	3.0
Saudi Arabia	11.1	10,530	5.9
Japan	120.0	10,630	4.7
Germany, Fed. Rep.	61.2	11,130	2.7
Sweden	8.3	11,860	1.8

Source: WB, *World Development Report 1986*, pp. 180–81, table 1.

99

in 1984/5 1.27 million and 682,000, respectively.[1] The number of students acquiring professional and technical training has also grown. By contrast, education along Western lines did not begin in Saudi Arabia until the 1960s, and for all the development that has occurred in this area in the last two decades, the gap between Egypt and Saudi Arabia is still enormous in this respect.

Egypt, then, was poor in capital assets and rich in human resources (poor-rich), while Saudi Arabia was rich in capital and poor in human resources (rich-poor). From the early 1960s onward, the three contrasting areas outlined above greatly affected the nature and course of relations between Egypt and Saudi Arabia, specifically between Nasser and his successors on the one hand and the rulers of the Saudi dynasty on the other. Notably, the relationship was characterized by extreme shifts, from political and military confrontation in the years 1962–67 to "cold cooperation" in the period between the wars of 1967 and 1973; and from close economic ties and wide-ranging Saudi aid in the years 1973–78 to the virtual termination of aid and the crystallization of a new mode of economic relations from 1979 until the mid-1980s.

THE NASSER YEARS

Egypt under Nasser advocated the idea of Arab unity. Yet the severe blow he suffered when the Syrians decided to dismantle the United Arab Republic in September 1961, together with other assaults on his leadership position in inter-Arab relations in the late 1950s and early 1960s, led to a rethinking of the ways and means to attain the unity he desired. Against this background, and for additional considerations as well, Nasser decided in October 1962 to dispatch an Egyptian expeditionary force to Yemen with the objective of assisting a group of army officers that had carried out a coup in San'a a month before to establish its rule over all parts of the country. Such help was needed in light of the serious and persistent opposition of the royal dynasty, supported by most of the tribes as well as by the Saudi rulers, who were providing financial and military backing.

Nasser and his advisers never anticipated the kind of morass into which their country's army and economy would sink as a result of this step. What began as a limited operation intended to last no more than a few weeks turned into a full-scale war, the longest that Egypt under Nasser was ever to know, with the provision of military support to one of the two armed camps in Yemen — the "republican" camp — rapidly turning into a military confrontation with Saudi Arabia itself. By November 1962, a month after the arrival of the Egyptian forces, the Egyptian air force was bombing villages and encampments of tribes living in Saudi territory near the Yemeni border, and soon thereafter began bombing villages and towns deep within the Saudi kingdom. The air raids continued intermittently throughout the five years of the conflict, the final attacks on Najran and Jizan drawing international attention. Saudi Arabia promptly broke off diplomatic relations with Egypt, in November 1962, and in June 1963 submitted an official complaint to the United Nations Security Council over the bombing of its civilian population.[2]

While the Egyptian military operations against Saudi Arabia did not develop into full-scale war between the two countries, undoubtedly, the presence of the Egyptian expeditionary force in Yemen for over five years (from October 1962 to December 1967) constituted a real threat to the stability of the Saudi regime. This was so due to a combination of three factors: (1) the negation by Nasser of the very legitimacy of the Saudi regime because of its "reactionary" character, and his insistence that it be replaced by a more "progressive" regime; (2) the presence of an Egyptian army numbering 40,000–70,000 troops for most of its period of intervention in Yemen;[3] and (3) the military weakness of the Saudis in contrast to the Egyptian army. Under these circumstances, the Saudis feared not only larger-scale Egyptian military operations, but also the encouragement that Saudi opposition groups drew from the military and political situation to act against the regime. Moreover, the Saudi government was afraid of revolutionary forces, with the direct or indirect support of Egypt, gaining control over other states in the Arabian Peninsula. To prevent such a development, the Saudis hurried to obtain American guarantees for the security of the monarchy in the face of aggressive acts from outside, while also adopting a comprehensive plan to enlarge their army and equip it with advanced weapons.

The war in Yemen cost Egypt dearly in economic resources. During the first part of the intervention, in 1962–65, the country was engrossed in an attempt at massive development (the first Five-Year Plan) financed by substantial foreign loans that created an external debt amounting to $2 billion by 1965.[4] A strenuous effort was needed to pay for the presence and operation of the Egyptian forces in Yemen by the second part of this period, in

1966–67, and the cost was particularly high: Egypt was obliged to halt its extensive investment program and cancel the second Five-Year Plan (1965–70) due to its inability to mobilize the capital required. The reduction in investment and productivity also resulted in a steep decline in economic growth rates. In 1966 the GNP rose by 0.6 percent only, while in 1967 it declined by 1.4 percent.[5] In addition, there were other costs to Egypt arising out of the intervention and the inability of the army to force a decisive outcome: human casualties, damage to the condition and morale of the army, and harm to the prestige of the regime at home and abroad, particularly in the inter-Arab sphere.

Why, then, did Nasser not seek a way out of Yemen when the economic, political and military costs of his remaining there became obvious? Conceivably, he did indeed search for an escape route before 1967, but any move of that sort would have been interpreted as an admission of failure by the Egyptian leadership, and this is at a time when Nasser's position and prestige in the Arab world were far from their strongest. Presumably, too, he was tenacious in his hope that the foothold he had obtained in Yemen would enable him to play a role in determining the future of the southern Arabian Peninsula and the Persian Gulf region. These aspirations were especially significant in view of the anticipated changes in the region with the completion of the withdrawal of British forces at the end of the 1960s. Furthermore, political power in the region was likely to bring with it additional economic rewards, namely the procurement of a share of the oil revenues that flowed into the coffers of some of the rulers in the Arabian Peninsula.[6]

In 1964, shortly before Egypt's development plan ground to a halt, a group of Egyptian economists was studying ways by which Egypt might benefit from resources at the disposal of other Arab states.[7] In the late 1960s the Egyptian government began to encourage the emigration of fellahin to several Arab countries.[8] The standstill in Egyptian economic growth and the accompanying hardships at home, combined with Nasser's interest in turning other Arab economic resources to Egypt's advantage as well as his desire to play a role in determining the future of the Arabian Peninsula, support the view that the Egyptian effort in Yemen was not devoid of economic considerations.

In May 1967 Nasser activated the other foreign arena in which his country was involved — Israeli-Egyptian-Arab relations — which had been quiescent since the end of the 1956 war. Nasser hoped that success in this arena would both help revive the process of economic growth in Egypt and bring the military deadlock in the Yemeni sands to an end. However, these efforts did not meet with success either.

One of the immediate effects of Egypt's defeat in the 1967 war was a further deterioration of its economic situation. The economy, already heavily mired in foreign debt, showing a severe deficit in its balance of trade, and in effect having stopped growing since 1965, suffered three more serious blows as a result of the war. First, several avenues for bringing in valuable foreign currency to the Egyptian treasury were closed off: the Suez Canal, which Nasser ordered blocked, the oil wells in Sinai, which fell to the Israelis, and tourism, whose revenues abruptly declined. The estimated total value of income from these sources in the year preceding the war was £E 213 million (1967 prices).[9] Second, military expenditure increased absolutely and relatively. The presence of the Israeli army on the banks of the Suez Canal brought the conflict with Israel to Egypt's doorstep, prompting Nasser to allocate ever larger sums to his army and to a projected renewal of the war. The share of military expenditure in the total GDP in the years 1967–70 rose from 13.2 percent to 18 percent.[10] Lastly, the War of Attrition that was waged during 1968–70 dislocated economic activity, hitting particularly hard at the cities along the Suez Canal. The industrial complexes that had been built there were totally destroyed and their citizens fled to Cairo and other major cities.

The need for available economic resources to feed the population and finance the war against Israel steadily increased following June 1967. However, under the regional and international circumstances of the late 1960s, additional economic aid was not available even from the Soviet Union, let alone the United States. A volte-face in Saudi Arabian relations occurred against this background. Shortly after the termination of the June war, the Saudis expressed their readiness to extend aid to Egypt. This gesture by a regime that regarded Nasser's Egypt as a bitter enemy is comprehensible in light of the double-edged sword under which the aid was given. The terms of the aid were that, on the one hand, Egypt was to cease its military and political activities against the Saudi and other monarchies in the Arabian Peninsula, with a withdrawal of its army from Yemen clearly implied. On the other hand, Egypt was obliged to continue the armed struggle against Israel. For the Saudis, the 1967 war and Egypt's concomitant economic difficulties provided a golden opportunity to change the course of developments in the Arabian Peninsula, while for Nasser the request for Saudi aid, and a later plea that this aid be enlarged, reflected a fundamental and painful change in his inter-Arab standing and in his policy. Nasser was forced to accept the Saudi *diktat*. By the end of 1967, he had completed the withdrawal of his expeditionary force from Yemen, while his propaganda attacks against the Saudi and other monarchs in the Arabian Peninsula ceased as well.

Moreover, Nasser was obliged to cooperate with the Saudi rulers in their vigorous efforts to strengthen their position at home and abroad, for example by agreeing to participate in the Islamic summit conference held in Rabat in September 1969. The fact that the conference was convened at all reflected the erosion in Egypt's standing generally and in Nasser's leadership position in particular. At the end of 1969 he was forced by economic plight to try to persuade the Saudis and the other Arab oil rulers to enlarge the aid they were extending to Egypt, an issue that was the focus of the fifth Arab summit conference held in December 1969 also in Rabat.[11] The discussions and resolutions reflected an element that was to become a conspicuous feature of the aid given by the Arab oil states to Egypt: it was granted first and foremost to finance the continuation of the war against Israel, that is, to equip and train the army. No aid was forthcoming at that stage to finance development projects or current economic needs. The military purpose of the aid was indicated in a variety of ways by the oil states, in particular Saudi Arabia. For example, at the annual conference of the Arab League in September 1968 Saudi Arabia (together with Libya) demanded that Egypt submit a detailed account of the uses to which the aid had been put. That same month Saudi Arabia, together with all the oil states providing aid to Egypt, decided that payments for military hardware would be made directly to the foreign banks through which the acquisitions were made. This move was intended to prevent any possible utilization of the funds by Egypt (and Jordan as well) for civilian goals not directly linked to the war against Israel.[12]

A CHANGING RELATIONSHIP

During the three years between Nasser's death (September 1970) and the October war, a change occurred in the amount of aid extended to Egypt, although not in its purpose. A series of factors contributed to Sadat succeeding in raising the aid level where Nasser had failed, namely: Egypt's weakened economy, the decline in its position in the Arab world, the end of the threat against the stability of the Saudi regime, and intensified preparations to renew the war against Israel, especially after the failure of the Jarring initiative in 1972. The amount of aid that Saudi rulers offered Sadat to finance military acquisitions increased during the year preceding the October war.[13] However, despite the proximity of the Egyptian and the Saudi positions, no change occurred in the conditions of the aid. The Saudis designated one purpose only for the money they gave — a war against Israel. Even Egypt's deteriorating economic situation did not change their approach. In 1973 the deficit in Egypt's balance of payments and the dearth of foreign currency worsened, with the import of basic food commodities in jeopardy. Sadat was not exaggerating in October 1973 when he stated that there were times when the country was left with only a few days' supply of wheat and barley.[14]

The October war altered Saudi aid in two important respects: (1) the amount of aid made available to Egypt increased immediately after the war; and (2) for the first time since Saudi Arabia began extending aid to Egypt, it was willing to grant considerable sums as civil aid toward the reconstruction of the Egyptian economy and toward foreign debt repayment. While military aid continued to be an important component in the total Saudi aid package, it no longer constituted the major part as it had in the period between the wars of 1967 and 1973. However, the increase in the quantity of aid did not continue for long. Peaking in 1974 and 1975, it fell steeply the following year.[15]

Rising oil revenues in the Middle East oil states, especially in Saudi Arabia, resulting in the accumulation of enormous monetary reserves — $150 billion in 1976[16] — prompted the Egyptian leadership to project a more organized and systematic framework for the long-term mobilization of funds. In 1975 Sadat proposed that the Arab oil states of the Persian Gulf finance a "Marshall Plan" for the development of the Egyptian economy. The figure mentioned for total investment was $10–12 billion, most of which would come from Saudi Arabia.[17] In July 1976 four Arab oil states — Saudi Arabia, Kuwait, the United Arab Emirates and Qatar — announced the establishment of a special fund, *hay'at al-khalij li'l-tanmiya fi misr*, or the Gulf Organization for the Development of Egypt (GODE). This time the aid was not earmarked for acquiring military hardware or covering current military expenditure, but was intended entirely for the purpose of financing development projects in Egypt. However, the establishment of GODE proved to be a disappointment for Egypt, which had hoped to receive approximately $2-2.5 billion a year. The GODE trustees resolved to underwrite only $2 billion for a period of five years, or an average of $400 million a year.[18]

Furthermore, the nature of the aid (not grants, but rather loans at the usual interest rates on the world money market), the conditions it entailed (reforms in the Egyptian economy as recommended by the International Monetary Fund), and statements made by the rulers of the GODE member states, conveyed the message to Egypt's leaders that economic aid on the order of billions of dollars annually over a long period could not be expected. Egyptian disappointment with the aid provided was great, not only because of the exacting conditions that came with it, the paltry sums actually extended, and the humiliating attitude shown toward Egypt's economic planners, but mainly on account of what could be read into the resolution of July 1976: the Arab oil states had no genuine interest in Egypt's economic reconstruction. Sadat grasped that Arab economic aid to Egypt was nearing its end.

It was against this background of dwindling Arab economic aid, increasingly pressing economic needs, and a leadership striving to sustain the process of reconstruction and economic growth that had begun following the 1973 war, that the "food riots" erupted in Egypt on 18-19 January 1977. The primary importance of the riots for the present discussion is that for the first time since the 1952 revolution, economic conditions threatened the very existence of the regime. Sadat understood that political stability would necessitate an uninterrupted process of reconstruction. This, in turn, would require, among other things, the import of a considerable amount of capital, free, moreover, of conditions that might jeopardize economic achievement. Sadat was able to test an alternative to Arab aid: financial assistance from the United States, other Western countries and Japan, as well as from international institutions such as the World Bank and the International Monetary Fund. This move proved to be most successful for three principal reasons.

First, the aid from the United States in the period 1981-85 amounted to an average of $2.4 billion annually.[19] Second, American aid was tendered in a regular fashion so that Egyptian planners could count on the exact sum once the annual US budget was approved. This was in contrast to Arab aid, which was usually disbursed in an unplanned and irregular way. Third, and perhaps most important, whereas Saudi aid was conditional on Egypt's continued active involvement in the Arab-Israeli conflict, if not as the leader of the Arab cause then at least as an important partner, US aid was conditional on Egypt's retirement from the conflict. In practical terms, American aid increased substantially after Egypt not only abandoned the conflict but signed a peace agreement with Israel. This suited the main thrust of Sadat's policy: to withdraw from the conflict and devote all available means to the economic development of Egypt, particularly the encouragement of foreign investment, the development of the oil sector, the expansion of tourism and the widening of the Suez Canal. None of these was consistent with continued active involvement in the conflict, not to mention that any gains accruing from Saudi or inter-Arab aid would have soon been lost through direct or indirect damage resulting from a renewal of hostilities with Israel.[20]

An important question in a discussion of Saudi-Egyptian relations in the 1970s is why the Saudi rulers rejected Egyptian requests in 1976 for expanded long-term economic aid, especially since Saudi refusal to extend massive aid was a major catalyst for Sadat's peace initiative. On the basis of material published both in Egypt and in Saudi Arabia, two explanations are plausible. One is that the Saudis, estimating that Egypt needed considerable economic assistance over the long term — $2–3 billion a year as a starting point — were apparently unwilling to make a commitment of this order. Alternatively, the Saudis might have been concerned that comprehensive aid would free the Egyptian leadership from focusing on economic and social reconstruction and allow Egypt to resume political activity in the Arab world along the lines of the early 1960s — a development the Saudis obviously wished to prevent.

Following Sadat's peace initiative in November 1977, a new pattern emerged in Saudi-Egyptian relations. Economic aid, rapidly decreasing during 1978, ceased entirely in 1979. In terms of military aid, a meager amount was granted by Saudi Arabia even after the signing of the Camp David Accords in September 1978, but no substantial aid was made available from 1979 onward. From then on, the United States replaced Saudi Arabia and the other oil states of the Arabian Peninsula as the primary supplier of both economic and military aid to Egypt. By contrast, aside from a brief period during 1979–80, there was no decline in other aspects of the economic relationship, namely the import and export of goods between Saudi Arabia and Egypt, Saudi tourism to Egypt, and Saudi deposits in Egyptian banks.[21] Furthermore, there was a marked rise in the number of Egyptian workers employed in the Saudi economy — from 50,000 in 1978 to 800,000 in 1982.[22] A new, more balanced economic relationship between the two countries took shape in the 1980s, therefore, based on mutual interest and involving the movement of manpower and capital between them.

CONCLUSION

The relationship between the two major countries on either side of the Red Sea basin during a period of a generation underwent significant upheavals: from Saudi responsiveness to Nasser's leadership in the inter-Arab arena in the mid-1950s to a serious political conflict that acquired the features of an armed clash, and from large-scale aid supplied by Saudi Arabia to Egypt in ever-increasing amounts, first only for military but later for economic purposes, to the halting of all such aid and the development of interdependent economic ties. The explanation for such extreme shifts in a relatively short period of time involves four different factors. The first was Nasser's ambition to establish a leading position for Egypt in the Arab world, which entailed, among other things, the propagation of Arab unity with Egypt at the center. The second factor was the leading role that Egypt played in the Arab-Israeli conflict. Third, the Egyptian economy experienced a crisis and was dependent on external sources in order to maintain growth at high rates over long periods. The last factor was Saudi Arabia's vast economic resources, resulting from the increase in revenues gained through the export of oil.

Egypt's confrontation with the Saudi regime in the 1960s, which resulted first and foremost from its intense involvement in Yemen, stemmed from its inter-Arab policy following the collapse of the United Arab Republic. The Yemen venture was intended to reinforce Egypt's leadership, at least in the "progressive camp," and its purpose was undoubtedly to suppress royalist forces not only in Yemen but in several other polities in the Arabian Peninsula. Additionally, it may be reasonably assumed that Nasser persisted in Yemen for so long in the hope that this intervention would eventually provide him with direct or indirect access to some of the oil resources of the Arabian Peninsula and the Persian Gulf. The war, however, brought Egypt no economic assets. On the contrary, it necessitated a heavy financial outlay and constituted a serious burden. Furthermore, the continued confrontation with the Saudis led to punitive measures by the United States, with American economic aid to Egypt declining drastically in 1964.[23]

The deadlock in the war in Yemen was accompanied by a prolonged standstill in the economic development of Egypt. The high rates of economic growth of the early 1960s ceased. Furthermore, the burden of foreign debt began to create a financial strain, with Egypt having increasing difficulty in sustaining repayment. Pressed by these difficulties, Nasser turned to the arena in which he had been active in the early years of his rule, that of the Arab-Israeli conflict, a move intended to break the deadlock and improve his leverage in mobilizing capital. However, what had been planned as a brilliant strategic ploy escalated to war and bitter military defeat in 1967.

The situation in which Nasser found himself after the 1967 war was insupportable: the Egyptian army was engaged in military confrontations on two fronts hundreds of miles apart — Yemen and the banks of the Suez Canal. This dual struggle had to be borne by an economy that even before the opening of an active second front against Israel was buckling under the burden that it carried. It was evident that war could not be conducted in both arenas, and that if continued operations were feasible on one front alone, it would have to be that of Israel rather than Yemen, for the obvious reason that Israel constituted the greater threat militarily and politically to the Nasser regime. However, the pursuit of the struggle against Israel demanded additional economic resources, both to repair war damage and to continue the armed conflict. For the first time since the 1952 revolution, Nasser needed urgent economic aid from the Arab states. The Saudis were willing to extend this aid on two conditions: withdrawal from Yemen and the complete termination of subversion against its regime; and a commitment to carry on the struggle against Israel, using Saudi aid toward this end exclusively. The link between Saudi aid and Egyptian military operations was especially pronounced during the period between the two Arab-Israeli wars of 1967 and 1973, in particular during 1972.

A new relationship developed between Egypt and Saudi Arabia

after the October war, one manifestation of which was a change in the amount and nature of aid required: the sums were measured in billions rather than millions of dollars, and the aid was earmarked for civil as well as military purposes. However, as it became increasingly obvious that Egypt under Sadat was planning to decrease its intense involvement in the Arab-Israeli conflict, Saudi support began to lose its momentum. Aid tapered off two years after the end of the war, and in the year that followed the Saudis made it clear that the period of generous assistance had in fact come to an end. The establishment of GODE in July 1976 reinforced this harsh reality, and even the food riots in January 1977 did nothing to alter the situation. Sadat was left without any doubt that aid was directly related to the degree of Egyptian involvement in the struggle with Israel.

By then, however, the option of Saudi and Arab aid at the price of permanent war with Israel was unattractive to Egypt, for it meant the continued ups and downs of construction and destruction that had been Egypt's lot until 1973. Sadat sought a different alternative: the recruitment of capital for rebuilding the Egyptian economy without jeopardizing economic achievements by a commitment to pursue war with Israel. The United States offered just such an opportunity, although Washington wanted more than nonbelligerency. Sadat was willing to comply, thereby breaking the bond that had existed since the mid-1950s, and especially after 1967, between the mobilization of economic resources for the Egyptian economy and intense involvement in the conflict with Israel. If the 1967 war signified the withdrawal of Egypt from its struggle against Saudi Arabia, the 1973 war signified the start of Egypt's virtual withdrawal from the conflict with Israel. In both these developments, economic factors played a major role.

The years following the peace agreement between Egypt and Israel (1979) are especially interesting in terms of Saudi-Egyptian relations. For the first time, an economic relationship was created on the basis of mutual interest, that is, a clear connection was established between Saudi and Egyptian economic needs. Saudi Arabia's increased oil export revenues and increased investment in its economic development led to a rise in demand for Egyptian workers and increased foreign currency transferred to Egypt. Conversely, the sharp fall in oil revenues and the reduction of the scope of investment in the Saudi economy jeopardized the jobs of many Egyptian workers there later on. There was also a clear, though not entirely direct, relationship between income from Saudi tourism and Saudi investment in Egypt, and the economic condition of Saudi Arabia itself.

More broadly, the nature of relations between Egypt and Saudi Arabia over 23 years greatly influenced Egypt's activity in the Arab arena and its involvement in the Arab-Israeli conflict. It was Saudi policy, inter alia, that led Egypt to abandon its efforts to play a central role in the attempt to foster Arab unity. Saudi Arabian policy was also one of the causes of Sadat's volte-face in terms of removing Egypt from the Arab-Israeli conflict. Egypt's turn inward in its quest for comprehensive economic reconstruction and sustained economic growth on the one hand, and economic developments in Saudi Arabia during the 1960s and 1970s on the other, constituted major forces in shaping the Middle East in the concluding decades of the twentieth century.

NOTES

1. CAPMAS, *SY 1986*, pp. 188, 201. See also Gad G. Gilbar, *The Middle East Oil Decade and Beyond*, London: Frank Cass, 1996, p. 79, table 5.1.
2. On the Yemen War, see Manfred W. Wenner, *Modern Yemen 1918–1966*, Baltimore: Johns Hopkins Press, 1967 (hereafter: Wenner); D.A. Schmidt, *Yemen: The Unknown War*, London: Bodley Head, 1968; Claude Deffarge and Gordian Troeller, *Yemen 62–69*, Paris: Editions Robert Lassont, 1969; Edgar O'Ballance, *The War in the Yemen*, London: Faber and Faber, 1971. (hereafter: O'Ballance).
3. Wenner, p. 210; O'Ballance, p. 155.
4. Ikram, p. 357.
5. Ibid., p. 398.
6. See, e.g., *al-Ahram*, 23, 26 February 1967.
7. Anouar Abdel-Malek, *Egypt: Military Society*, New York: Vintage Books, 1968, pp. 285–87.
8. *al-Ahram*, 18 December 1967.
9. Waterbury, *Nasser and Sadat*, p. 415.
10. Kanovsky, pp. 288–89.
11. Avraham Sela, *Ahdut be-tokh perud ba-ma'arekhet ha-beyn 'arvit*, Jerusalem: Magnes Press, 1982, pp. 88–91, 94–95.
12. Ibid., p. 82.
13. EIU, *Quarterly Economic Review, Egypt*, nos. 3, 4 (1973), no. 2 (1975).
14. *al-Usbu' al-'Arabi*, 8 October 1974.
15. For data on Saudi aid to Egypt, see J. M. Wien, *Saudi-Egyptian Relations: The Political and Military Dimensions of Saudi Financial Flows to Egypt*, Santa Monica, Calif.: RAND, 1980, pp. 47–60.
16. For data on the monetary reserves of the Arab oil countries dring 1974–84, see OAPEC, *Secretary General's Eighth Annual Report 1981*, Kuwait, 1982, p. 66; IMF, *World Economic Outlook 1983*, Washington, D.C., 1983, p. 187; *PE* (June 1985): 196.
17. *al-Ahram*, 22 May 1975; MENA, 26 July 1976.
18. *MEED*, 7 May 1976, p. 17; Ikram, pp. 345–46, 364.
19. USAID, *U.S. Overseas Loans and Grants from International Organizations*,

Obligations and Loan Authorizations, Washington D.C., 1985 (hereafter: UDAID, *Overseas Loans and grants*).

20. Gad Gilbar, "Egypt's Economy: The Challenge of Peace," *Jerusalem Quarterly* 12 (1979): 8-9.
21. IMF, *Direction of Trade Statistics, Yearbook 1985*, p. 164; Government of Egypt, General Authority for the Promotion of Tourism, *Tourist Statistical Information 1975-1984*, Cairo, 1985.
22. *al-Ahram*, 18 September 1978, 12 October 1983. See also Gil Feiler, "The Number of Egyptian Workers in the Arab Oil Countries, 1974-1983: A Critical Discussion," *Occasional Papers*, no. 96, Tel Aviv: Dayan Center for Middle Eastern and African Studies, 1986, pp. 22-23.
23. USAID, *Overseas Loans and Grants*, 1975.

7

Family Planning under Mubarak

INTRODUCTION

The official estimate of the population of Egypt in mid-1992 was 58.2 million,[1] of which 56.5 million resided in Egypt itself and the rest lived abroad.[2] From the time that Husni Mubarak was inaugurated as president of Egypt in October 1981 until the end of 1992, the population of Egypt grew by 15.2 million inhabitants, an increase of about 35 percent (see table 7.1). According to most forecasts, the population of Egypt at the end of the 1990s will have increased by over three times its size at the time of the July 1952 revolution.[3]

This population growth was the outcome of a sharp rise in the rate of natural increase from the early 1970s until the late 1980s, from an average of 21.3 per thousand during 1968–72 to an average of 29.1 per thousand during 1984–88 (see table 7.2). However, a shift in the level of natural increase occurred in 1989. Official reports for 1989–92 cite rates which are substantially lower than those for the 1974–88 period: the average rate of crude natural increase for the years 1989–92 was 23.7 per thousand (see table 7.2). As a result of this drop, annual natural increase in absolute terms was halted and even reversed.

The decline of the natural increase rate during 1989–92 was the result of a distinct decrease in the crude birthrate. These rates dropped from an average level of 38.2 per thousand in 1984–88 to an average level of 31.2 per thousand in 1989–92. The effect of the drop in the crude birthrate, however, was mitigated somewhat

113

Table 7.1

Egypt: midyear population estimates, number of births and deaths, and natural increase, 1952, 1960, 1966, 1976 and 1981–92
(in thousands)

	Total population	Births	Deaths	Natural increase
1952	21,437	969	381	588
1960	25,960	1,114	438	676
1966	30,188	1,235	477	758
1976	37,858	1,384	445	939
1981	43,322	1,604	434	1,170
1982	44,506	1,612	444	1,168
1983	45,721	1,684	445	1,239
1984	46,900	1,815	447	1,368
1985	48,349	1,922	456	1,466
1986	49,864	1,928	458	1,470
1987	51,349	1,923	468	1,455
1988	52,827	1,923	429	1,504
1989	54,210	1,743	417	1,326
1990[a]	55,543	1,807	415	1,392
1991[a]	56,898	1,761	430	1,331
1992[a]	58,194	1,698	432	1,266

Note:
a   Provisional.

Sources:
1952–76: CAPMAS *SY 1992*, p. 26, table. 1–16.
1981–92: CAPMAS *SY 1993*, p. 28, table 1–18.

by the continued reduction in the crude death rate, which decreased from an average level of 9.1 per thousand during 1984–88 to 7.6 per thousand in 1989–92. The infant mortality rate (up to the age of 1 year) was also reduced, from 94 deaths per thousand live births in 1984 to 66 deaths in 1990.[4]

The changes in the birthrate during the late 1980s reflect the sharp decline in the total fertility rate of Egyptian women in that period. For many years (1976–82), this rate had remained stable at a level of 5.3 children. A slow decrease in the fertility rate began in 1983, with a dramatic change occurring in 1988–90 when the rate dropped from 4.7 to 4.0.[5]

114

Table 7.2

Egypt: birth, death and natural increase rates, 1953–92
(per thousand)

	Crude birthrate	Crude death rate	Crude natural increase rate
1953–57	40.8	17.6	23.2
1958–62	42.4	16.7	25.7
1963–67	41.4	15.1	26.3
1968–72	36.0	14.7	21.3
1973–77	36.3	12.3	24.0
1978–82	37.7	10.3	27.4
1983	36.8	9.7	27.1
1984	38.6	9.5	29.1
1985	39.8	9.4	30.4
1986	38.7	9.2	29.5
1987	37.4	9.1	28.3
1988	36.6	8.1	28.5
1989	32.2	7.7	24.5
1990[a]	32.5	7.5	25.0
1991[a]	31.0	7.6	23.4
1992[a]	29.2	7.4	21.8

Note:
a   Provisional.
Sources:
1953–82: Jumhuriyyat misr al-'arabiyya, al-jihaz al-markazi lil-ta'bi'a al-'amma wal-ihsa, *al-Kitab al-ihsa'i al-sanawi 1952–1980*, Cairo: al-Jihaz, 1982, p. 20.
1983–92: CAPMAS *SY 1993*, p. 28, table 1–18.

Notably, there were pronounced differences in fertility rates between different groups in Egypt. A fertility survey conducted in 1988 shows that the lowest rates were found in the urban provinces (Cairo, Alexandria, Port Said and Suez), while the highest rates were in the rural provinces in Upper Egypt. The gap was very large: 3.27 children in the urban provinces compared with 6.44 in the rural areas.[6] Data for 1975–88 illustrate the large gap in levels of fertility between the urban and rural populations (especially the villages of Upper Egypt). While the fertility rate in the urban population dropped from an average of 5.87 in 1975–80 to 4.40 in 1983–88, the rate in the rural districts of Upper Egypt rose during that period from 6.32 to 6.44.[7]

Figure 7.1
Egypt: total population, 1970-92

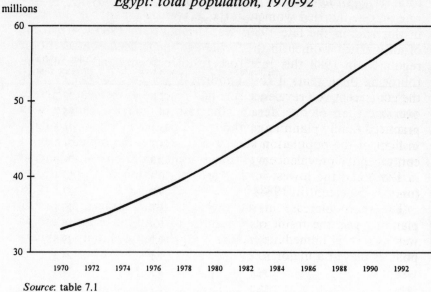

Source: table 7.1

Figure 7.2
Egypt: birthrate and death rate, 1970-92

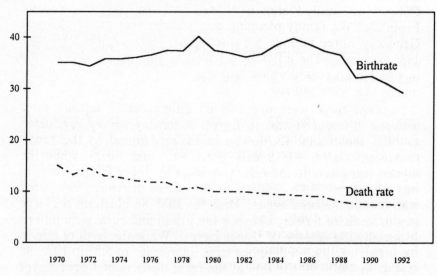

Source: table 7.2

One of the immediate factors accounting for the drop in the total fertility rate was the increase in the contraceptive prevalence rate among married women in the fertile age range. The increase in this rate in the late 1980s was dramatic: in 1980, 24 percent of all married women in the fertile age range used contraception regularly, in 1988 this rate rose to 38 percent, and during the following three years it rose another 10 percent, so that by 1991 the contraceptive prevalence rate had reached 48 percent.[8] Hence, over the span of one decade, the rate of married women who practiced family planning methods had doubled. Not surprisingly, in light of the population survey cited above, the highest rate of contraceptive prevalence was found in the major cities (56 percent in 1988) and the lowest in the rural population of Upper Egypt (only 11.5 percent in 1988).[9]

The sharp increase in the rate of families practicing family planning was the result of a number of long-range processes as well as several immediate factors.[10] Of the latter, family planning policies played a major role.

STAGES IN EGYPT'S FAMILY PLANNING POLICY

Egypt was the first Arab country in the Middle East to adopt a family planning policy. The application of this policy began in December 1965, when the Egyptian government set up the Supreme Council for Family Planning (al-Majlis al-a'la li-tanzim al-usra). From then on, family planning policy underwent major changes. Generally, three periods are discernible: 1965-72, 1973-84, and 1985 onward.[11] The differences between these periods lay mainly in orientation regarding the application of the policy and in the means that were utilized.

The first stage, 1965-72: The direct, supply-oriented approach. Family planning policy makers during the latter part of Nasser's rule adopted the direct-approach policy, with activity focused on the supply side, which reflected the dominant attitude in international bodies, especially the Population Council, which was active in introducing family planning policies to Third World countries in the 1960s. This approach held that it was possible to bring about a rapid decrease in fertility rates in developing countries by supplying the population with inexpensive contraceptives and readily available abortion services. While the Egyptian government rejected the abortion component, demographic-policy makers in

117

the second half of the 1960s adopted the premise that easy access to the necessary information and to contraceptives (principally pills and IUDs) would prompt married couples to practice family planning. The assumption by the authorities in Egypt, as in other developing countries, was that married couples in the fertile age range were interested, a priori, in having a small family (three to four children), so that supplying information and means would bring about a reduction in the fertility rate.[12]

A convenient way of putting this approach into practice was devised by utilizing the widespread health network, namely, the mother and child clinics and stations operated by the Ministry of Health. In 1966 family planning units were set up in these clinics, generally consisting of a doctor and a nurse who provided information and supplied contraceptives. Hence, a few months only after the actual implementation of the policy, the authorities announced that family planning services were available at 2,850 mother and child clinics throughout the country.[13]

However, the authorities were aware from the start that the supply approach alone was insufficient in order to bring about a change in the fertility rate, and that a change in the demand for family planning services was also needed. The demand approach held that in societies where traditional values prevailed among large sectors of the population, concerted efforts had to be made to convince couples of the inherent advantages of having a small family. In Egypt, as in other Islamic states, most 'ulama and most of the lower strata of society were opposed to antinatalist policy.

Following the introduction of family planning, the authorities made an attempt to weaken the influence of traditional norms that encouraged high fertility. Distinguished religious figures such as the Mufti of Egypt and Shaykh al-Azhar were persuaded to publish learned opinions asserting that family planning did not contradict Islamic law and that using birth control was not a religious offense. Indeed, fatwas, articles in Islamic periodicals and interviews in daily papers were published.[14] The government instructed rural and urban preachers employed by the Ministry of Awqaf to inform the public of these opinions, but it failed to achieve significant cooperation in this area, and many of the preachers, including those salaried by the government, resisted family planning and expressed explicit disapproval.[15]

At first glance, family planning appears to have achieved considerable success during 1965–72. The total fertility rate dropped from 6.8 in 1965 to 5.5 in 1972, while the crude birthrate dropped from 41.7 to 34.4 during the same period. Most impressive was the drop in the rates of crude natural increase, from 27.6 in 1965 to 19.9 in 1972.[16] Yet data on the contraceptive prevalence rate show that family planning policy was not the major factor accounting for the changes in fertility and natural increase. Fertility dropped despite only a minute change in the contraceptive prevalence rate.[17] There is reason to assume, therefore, that the war situation in Egypt during 1967–73, which involved large recruitment of men into the army along with a severe economic crisis, was the factor that brought about the reduction in fertility and birthrates.[18]

The second stage, 1973-84: The indirect approach. A slow, albeit undeclared, withdrawal from the direct, supply-oriented approach occurred during the first years of Sadat's rule. The name of the Supreme Council for Family Planning was changed in 1973 to the Supreme Council for Family Planning and Population *(al-Majlis al-a'la li-tanzim al-usra wal-sukan)*, reflecting a gradual transition from a direct to an indirect approach which reached its final form in 1977.

The motif of the indirect approach was "development is the best contraceptive." According to this approach, reduction of fertility would be achieved as a byproduct of extensive social and economic development, including an improvement in the income level and well-being of the individual; better social services, especially in education and health; and expanded employment opportunities for women and their integration into the labor force. While family planning services would be expanded, this aspect was no longer the focus of the antinatalist policy.[19]

The shift from a direct to an indirect approach in the 1970s had a largely political motivation. Sadat, wishing to broaden support for his regime, made efforts to establish new relationships with Islamic movements in Egypt during this period, especially with the Muslim Brethren.[20] These efforts, in Sadat's view, necessitated adopting an indirect approach to the reduction of fertility, that is, a policy which would not conflict with the position of the Muslim Brethren on reproduction. What made it possible to adopt this policy approach after 1974 was substantial capital import and a high rate of economic growth which lasted until 1984. Between 1975 and 1984 the GDP grew at an annual average rate of 8.1 percent.[21] The change in policy emphasis was reflected in particular in the government-initiated Population and Development Project in 1977, aimed primarily at the rural population, where the focus was on improving management performance in village institutions and on increasing the levels of education, especially of women.

Although the indirect approach had the advantage of avoiding conflict with a wide segment of the public opposed to antinatalist policy, its drawback was that even if the processes of economic and social development were accelerated, results in the area of reducing fertility rates would take many years to appear. In fact, crude birthrates and rates of natural increase in the late 1970s and in the first half of the 1980s not only failed to drop, they actually rose to the extent that by 1985, the rate of natural increase was the highest of the century and probably the highest ever in Egypt (30.4 per thousand).[22] It had become apparent in the early 1980s that even though the level of average income had increased in real terms, there was no reduction in the total fertility rate, which remained at 5.3 in 1983, exactly the same as it had been in 1976.[23]

With the abrupt halt in the growth of the Egyptian economy in the mid-1980s, hardship due to population increase intensified. It was clear that the indirect approach could no longer be pursued and that a pronounced change which would achieve actual results was required.

The third stage, 1985–92: The demand-oriented direct approach. The announcement by the government of the establishment of a National Population Council (*al-Majlis al-qawmi lil-sukan*) in January 1985[24] reflected yet another change in approach regarding government fertility policy. Although the new policy included elements from the first stage and, to a limited extent, from the second stage, it signified important changes in two areas: First, family planning policy was given high priority on the national agenda. While it had been on the fringes of socioeconomic policy under Nasser and Sadat, it became a central policy issue in the second half of the 1980s and the early 1990s. Second, while supply was to be improved, increasing demand received the highest priority. On the supply side, the government invested considerably in expanding the existing network of family planning clinics and stations, especially in rural areas. On the demand side, several means were used to influence married couples to limit their number of offspring.

120

THE NEW FAMILY PLANNING POLICY

Efforts to affect demand. Since 1985, the government has taken steps both on the national and the community level designed to change the attitude of couples who rejected or questioned the moral basis or the practical justification of family planning. Nationally, the following means were used:

a. Direct appeals by President Mubarak to the public on various occasions calling for the practice of birth control. His speeches on national commemorative days (e.g., Revolution Day, 1 May) were widely covered in the electronic and the print media.[25]

b. Public speeches and statements on the need to adopt family planning delivered by ministers and senior officials, including the ministers of health, welfare, agriculture, awqaf, education and information, as well as by the chairman of the National Population Council and the president of the Central Agency for Public Mobilization and Statistics.[26]

c. Fatwas, articles and interviews published in the media by leading Muslim and Coptic religious authorities (the Mufti, Shaykh al-Azhar and the Coptic patriarch), all avowing that there was no religious reason not to practice birth control.[27]

d. Articles and essays by well-known journalists portraying the negative results of the rapid population growth. These articles included forecasts of future population size and the enormous difficulties facing the country should high rates of natural increase be maintained.[28]

e. Easily understood short films ("commercials") on Egyptian television calling upon the public to have small families.[29]

f. Posters advocating small families displayed in government offices, reproduced in the press, and appearing on billboards in city squares and along highways.[30]

g. Caricatures in the newspapers, especially those that express government views, illustrating the phenomenon of population explosion and the consequences of rapid population growth in various areas (e.g., housing, services and employment).[31]

At the local community level the means utilized included:

a. Preachers employed by the Ministry of Awqaf propagating the message that family planning was permitted by Islamic religious law.[32]

b. Preachers (*du'at*) specially trained by the Ministry of Awqaf propagating the approval of established Islam concerning family planning in the villages.[33]

Illustration 7.1
*Madam Population Growth strangles Ms Development — Mr
Inflation is set free*

Source: al-Ahram, 17 September 1989

Illustration 7.2
Ms Development sits on a mine "population growth"

Source: *al-Ahram,* 24 January 1989

Illustration 7.3
Population Growth chasing Ms Development

Source: *al-Ahram,* 31 July 1988

Illustration 7.4
Population explosion: "Made in Egypt"
Source: *al-Ahram*, 10 September 1988

llustration 7.5
Ms Development threatens to drown
Source: *al-Ahram*, 23 January 1989

Illustration 7.6
Cairo bus: "Egypt 1"

Source: al-Ahram al-Iqtisadi, 17 February 1992

125

c. Women volunteers promoting the activities of the family planning clinics and stations in rural areas. The task of these volunteers, who themselves belonged to the rural community, was to locate women who already had a number of children (usually four or five) and persuade them not to extend their family further. The volunteers were backed up by professional staff in the family planning centers.[34]

The Expansion of Supply. The network of family planning services in the 1960s included three different components: governmental, voluntary public and private,[35] with the governmental component playing the major role. The government in fact initiated and controlled all the services, determining the limits of private sector activity as well. Not surprisingly, voluntary organizational activity undertaken to advance family planning was marginal. This dominant etatist element reflected not only the post-1952 revolution policy of direct control over economic and social activity, but also stemmed from the political and social sensitivity of the birth control issue in Egyptian society, which, in the government's view, could not be left in the hands of either the private sector or voluntary organizations.

The governmental system for providing services was composed of both regional centers and local clinics/stations. Some seven to eight regional family planning centers in each province (1990) coordinated the supply system and made efforts to stimulate demand.[36] Ongoing activity was maintained by local clinics or family planning units under the supervision of the Ministry of Health and other ministries. In 1991, 4,213 such family units were functioning in Egypt,[37] 63 percent of them in villages and 37 percent in towns.[38] These units were located in government hospitals, mother and child clinics, and special stations established by the Ministries of Social Affairs and Agriculture.[39] In 1991 the entire governmental system employed 5,604 doctors in full- and part-time positions, and 15,000 nurses.[40] The private component in the system encompassed over 4,400 privately owned pharmacies[41] which sold contraceptives, as well as private clinics offering family planning services located both in rural areas and in towns.[42] Voluntary organizations operated a small number of clinics, located mainly in the large cities.[43]

Field studies conducted in Egypt and elsewhere have shown that the availability of contraceptives is an important factor in an individual's decision to adopt family planning. Specifically, a

126

high degree of correlation was found between the contraceptive prevalence rate and the distance from the source of supply. The contraceptive prevalence rate was higher in locations where contraceptives were available within walking distance or a short drive away, as compared with locations where the distance was longer.[44]

A high degree of availability of contraceptives was apparently achieved in Egypt. A demographic survey conducted between October 1988 and January 1989 encompassing 9,805 households in 120 villages in Lower and Upper Egypt found that 64 percent of rural married women in the fertile age range had access to contraceptives in the villages where they lived (through public or private clinics or pharmacies), and 97 percent had access to birth control within 5 kilometers of their village.[45] Another significant finding was that 68 percent of the villages included in the survey had a specially trained family planning nurse.[46] The survey also showed, however, that the network of government services alone — the government family planning clinics — was insufficiently widespread and did not meet the high-availability criterion: 90 percent of the villages were up to 30 kilometers away from a public family planning clinic.[47] In light of this finding, the government continued to allocate resources for opening new family planning clinics and stations through 1992, as well as for training medical and paramedical personnel.[48] Government expenditure forecasts for family planning activity beyond 1992 showed a substantial increase in allocations both for expanding the family planning network and improving the quality of services offered by it.[49]

A Noncoercive Approach. Despite intensive efforts to bring about lower fertility rates, family planning policy during 1985–92 remained noncoercive and soft, manifested in two ways: (1) the policy was completely voluntary, without any element of direct or indirect coercion and without either negative or positive incentives; and (2) pronatalist elements were still retained in government policy, both directly and indirectly.

The approach of the Egyptian government was that the transition by a couple from reliance on "childbearing by nature," with the number of progeny dependent on biological factors only, to planning the size of the family, could be accomplished by persuasion as to the advantages of having a small family. Voluntary in nature, this policy also rejected the stick-and-carrot approach, that is, granting material rewards, or imposing financial or other punishments, to promote the transition to family planning.

Nevertheless, with pressure on resources as a result of rapid population growth becoming evident, the voluntary approach was increasingly criticized as failing to stem the demographic tide, and proposals to enhance motivation for birth control by reward or sanction were raised. Proposals to integrate negative incentives in the family planning policy included forcing couples with more than three or four children to pay for the education and health services of the fourth or fifth child onward.[50] More far-reaching was a proposal to offer a bonus to men willing to be sterilized.[51]

Mubarak, along with government ministers and officials involved with family planning policy, consistently resisted these pressures, arguing that the denial of services such as education and health to any citizen was in contradiction to the constitution.[52] There was no legal way of demanding payment for primary school education or medical care for a child no matter how many siblings he had. Moreover, such sanctions would be contrary to the principles of the government's social policy,[53] as they would first and foremost harm the weakest strata of the population, which had the largest families. Another consideration, which was not articulated, was the likelihood that the use of sanctions by the government would elicit severe opposition in wide sectors of the population, especially in the lower classes in the cities. As in other areas (e.g., subsidies, housing and employment), drawing up policy was based on an evaluation of the level of tolerance of the population, and primarily that of the masses in the major cities. Nevertheless, there were indications that the government was considering financial awards and other bonuses for couples who limited their families to two or three children. A limited experiment in this direction was made in several villages in the province of Fayyum in 1990,[54] although the conclusions drawn from it by the government were not publicized.

Government natalist policy, however, suffered from intrinsic contradictions. Significant direct and indirect pronatalist components were still part of Egyptian social policy in the early 1990s. For instance, the authorities continued to award certain tax exemptions and a reduction in income tax to large families, while salary bonuses in the public sector were still granted according to the number of children in the employee's family.[55]

The influence of pronatalist attitudes was also reflected in the lack of appropriate punitive steps taken against Egyptians who blatantly violated laws which could discourage high fertility. For example, the law stipulating a minimal marriage age (sixteen for women, eighteen for men) was consistently broken, but this disregard of regulations was viewed with tolerance. According to the 1986 census, 30 percent of first marriages in Egypt's rural districts involved an underage partner, usually the woman.[56] While there were indications that a certain drop in the rate of underage marriages occurred in the late 1980s, particularly in rural society, the phenomenon was still common,[57] abetted by the difficulty in enforcing the law because of the ingenious methods devised by the fellahin to circumvent it.[58]

Another area that influenced fertility rates was the widespread use of child labor, especially in the villages. According to official data for 1987, 1.5 million children (aged six to fifteen) were regularly employed by adult family members.[59] The contribution of working children to household income in the late 1980s was estimated at 20 percent of the average wage of an adult employee.[60] Enforcing the law in this area was difficult because from a legal viewpoint there was some question as to whether child labor was prohibited.[61]

These loopholes in the law and inconsistencies in its enforcement, combined with an entrenched tradition of large families, resulted in reduced effectiveness of the family planning effort. The regime, anxious to refrain from antagonizing the masses, tolerated these internal contradictions in its fertility policy.

Another indication of the government's self-imposed limit in enacting family planning policy was the total budgetary allocation for it. Total expenditure in 1988 for family planning, from both local and foreign sources, was £E 46 million,[62] slated to rise to £E 61 million by 1993.[63] Of total expenditure in 1988, over half (52 percent) came from external sources — grants by international organizations and foreign governments to further Egypt's family planning efforts[64] — while the Egyptian government contributed only 37 percent or £E 17 million.[65] Of Egypt's total 1988–89 budget of £E 21.7 billion,[66] social services (health and education) were allocated £E 3.1 billion,[67] so that the government's share in family planning expenditure was only 0.5 percent of the total social services budget and 3.1 percent of the public health budget. This allocation was modest both in absolute and relative terms. Significantly, the main reason did not seem to be a lack of resources, for had the government wished to intensify family planning efforts, additional funds from one or more of the foreign donors would have been available.

OPPOSITION TO FAMILY PLANNING POLICY

The opposition to Mubarak's antinatalist policy, particularly the Islamic movements, claimed that Egypt's economic problems — unemployment, lack of housing and inflation — were first and foremost the result of an inadequate governmental policy and misguided leadership rather than rapid population increase. In their view, the emphasis that the government put on the demographic factor was merely an attempt to find an excuse for its failure to bring about change and an improvement in the economy, particularly in the standard of living of the lower classes.[68] Both the Islamic and the right-wing opposition asserted that the solution to Egypt's hardships lay in sustained development and rapid economic growth. They claimed that Egypt's economic potential was not being realized, and that a suitable social and economic policy could satisfy the needs of the entire population.[69]

There was, however, an absence of unanimity on the part of the various groups opposing family planning policy. The new/old right, which had reorganized itself as the new Wafd Party, was unconvinced that an antinatalist policy could effect any basic change in the state of the economy and the society, and therefore opposed giving it priority or allocating resources to it. The secular right, however, did not fault the policy in terms of traditions or values.[70]

Moderate Islamic groupings with ties to the government, as well as the moderate wing of the Muslim Brethren, did not entirely reject family planning (*tanzim al-usra*), holding that since it was designed to allow a certain timespan between each birth for the protection of the health of the mother and her children, it was permitted by the Shari'a, as was the use of contraceptives for this purpose. However, restricting birth (*tahdid al-nasil*), that is, using contraceptives to prevent additional births after the second or third child, was forbidden by Islamic religious law. The basis of this approach was that the Shari'a did not recognize economic hardship as a reason for restricting family size. Children contributed to the wealth and well-being of the family and of society, according to the Islamic point of view, and every Muslim was required to have as many children as bestowed by Allah.[71]

Radical Islamic movements rejected any kind of interference

130

in the process of fertility, namely, birth restriction or family planning. Contraception was justified only when the life of the woman was endangered by pregnancy. Any other factor, such as general health considerations or poverty, was not recognized as valid. The radicals viewed family planning as extreme heresy that challenged the fundamentals of Islam, reiterating accusations voiced by opponents of family planning in the 1950s and 1960s that the adoption of this policy resulted from pressure exerted by infidels, first and foremost the United States, who feared a large and strong Egypt. In this view, the adoption and enactment of such a policy signified the surrender of Egypt's rulers to foreign pressures and reflected weakness rather than a response to reality.[72]

The coalition of forces opposed, in varying degrees, to family planning policy might not have been effective in restricting it to any significant extent were it not that these attitudes were held by large sectors of the population, especially in rural society. Egypt's rural society in the early 1990s still viewed having many children as a major asset, for three reasons. The first was related to the woman's interest: having many children reinforced the woman's position in the family. Conceivably, it was the most important element in determining her position and status vis-à-vis her husband, her husband's other wives, her husband's family generally and her mother-in-law in particular, and the community as a whole. Thus, women who did not acquire alternative sources of power (property ownership or a profession) strove to have many children.[73] The second reason related mainly to the man's perspective: children still constituted important aid in agricultural work and a contributing factor to family income.[74] The third reason was common to both husband and wife: adolescent children were still the most important, if not the only, support for the couple when they reached old age. As this responsibility was borne by male children only, generally at least two male children were needed. With child mortality still high, couples sought to have at least seven children so that they might have two sons to guarantee care in old age.[75] Significantly, there was no conflict between the position of the wife and the husband in this context: both wanted many children. This desire was perceived as basic for survival and went beyond religious and other traditional norms. Religious functionaries in the Egyptian *rif* (Egypt's rural area) essentially reflected the attitudes of the public which they served, to a great extent legitimizing rather than molding popular opinion.

CONCLUSION

The third stage in the history of family planning policy in Egypt (1985–92) did not contain any radical departures from the two previous stages, reflecting elements of continuity especially with the first stage (1965–72). Mubarak's regime adhered to a voluntary policy of birth control based on persuasion, lacking both negative and positive incentives, which did not cancel out existing direct or indirect pronatalist elements. The policy was etatist, with the state the main player in this arena, aided by the private sector (pharmacies, clinics and private donors) in the distribution of contraceptives.

Nevertheless, a significant difference in approach and implementation in several areas was adopted from 1985 onward, revealing a leap forward. Egypt developed a direct-approach family planning policy which attached great importance to the demand side, with the political leadership actively promoting a change of attitude toward fertility within the population. There was, however, criticism both from Egypt and abroad that the government was not doing enough. Demographic experts, scholars, journalists and even representatives in the People's Assembly (*Majlis al-sha'b*) urged the government to initiate more radical measures, such as the enactment, albeit gradual, of positive incentives or the withholding of certain services heretofore granted by the state to large families.

The question of why Mubarak did not employ more radical measures in this area, in light of his own statements that the issue was crucial to the future of Egypt, deserves consideration. For years the regime had been walking a tightrope with regard to its relationship with the Islamic opposition. The government also knew that the lower strata of Egyptian society perceived family planning as working against their interests and basic needs. The government, for its part, was ineffective in convincing the masses of rural and urbanized fellahin that having a small family could improve their own personal position.

Mubarak, as his predecessors in office ever since the Free Officers' Revolution, failed to elicit grass-roots support for the social and economic goals of the regime. Such a development might have counterbalanced the influence of the Islamic organizations on the issue of the population problem. However, in light of internal developments in Egypt in 1992–93, namely, the escalation of the struggle between the government and the radical Islamic

132

movements, it would appear that Mubarak knew better than his critics how far the government could go in implementing family planning policy.

Considering the restrictions with which the government contended, therefore, the sharp drop in fertility rates that occurred at the end of the 1980s should be regarded as a significant achievement. The implication of this development goes beyond the Egyptian context. It is apparently the first case in which a government succeeded in motivating a substantial part of the population to adopt family planning through voluntary measures alone. If the government can maintain this process in the years to come, the experiment could become a model for other Third World countries struggling with the phenomenon of rapid population growth and increasing pressure on resources, but unwilling or unable to institute a family planning policy based on a system of rewards (the Indian model) or coercion (the Chinese model). If it is indeed possible to effect real change in this area in a relatively short period of time by persuasion alone, then the process initiated in Egypt in 1985 may have far-reaching effects.

There were, however, no signs of satisfaction with the results of the natalist policy in Cairo in the early 1990s, reflecting a lack of confidence that the high rates of reduction in natural increase could be maintained. In fact, there was some doubt that the approach and techniques used to effect change at the end of the 1980s would suffice to sustain the process during the 1990s.[76] Targets established by Egyptian policy makers for 1999 were to increase the contraceptive prevalence rate from 48 percent to 60 percent, reduce the fertility rate from 4 to 3.1, and lower the rate of natural increase from 23 to 18 per thousand.[77]

Projected government activity focused on further expansion of supply and acceleration of demand for family planning services in rural areas, especially in Upper Egypt. Egypt's leaders were aware, however, that even if these goals of the fertility policy were achieved, the population would still grow by more than 1 million annually in the near future, i.e., that between 1993 and 1999 the population would increase by about 8 million. Hence, Mubarak and his government knew that whatever the achievements of the natalist policy, only substantial economic growth could bring about an improvement in the welfare of the population.

NOTES

1. CAPMAS, *SY 1993*, p. 28, table 1-18.
2. *MEED*, 31 July 1992.
3. UN, *World Population Prospects — 1992 Revision*, pp. 448-49; cf. UNDP, *Human Development Report 1992*, New York: Oxford University Press, 1992, p. 171, table 22; WB, *World Development Report 1992*, p. 268, table 26.
4. WB, *World Development Report 1986*, p. 232, table 27; *1992*, p. 272, table 28.
5. WB, *World Tables 1989-90*, Baltimore and London: Johns Hopkins University Press, 1990, pp. 226-27; id., *World Development Report 1992*, p. 270, table 27.
6. Ibrahim K.T. Osheba and Hussein A. Sayed, "The Fertility Impact of Contraceptive Use in Egypt: An Aggregate Analysis," Cairo Demographic Centre, *Working Paper*, no. 2, 1991, p. 11, table 1 (hereafter: Osheba and Sayed).
7. Ibid.
8. Ibrahim K.T. Osheba, "The Proximate Determinants of Fertility Change in the Regions of Egypt, 1980-88," Cairo Demographic Centre, *Working Paper*, no. 26, 1992, p. 5.
9. Osheba and Sayed, p. 16, table 3.
10. Richard A. Easterlin, Eileen M. Crimmins, Mohamed A. Ahmed and Samia M. Soliman, "The Impact of Modernization on the Motivation for Fertility Control," in Awad M. Hallouda, Samir Farid and Susan H. Cochrane (eds.), *Egypt, Demographic Responses to Modernization*, Cairo: CAPMAS, 1988, pp. 645-69.
11. For a different periodization, see: CAPMAS, *SY 1988*, pp. 5-6.
12. Saad M. Gadalla, *Is There Hope? Fertility and Family Planning in a Rural Egyptian Community*, Cairo: American University in Cairo Press, 1978, pp. 214-15; Charles E. Gallagher, "Population and Development in Egypt. Part II: New Hopes for Old Problems," *American University Field Staff Reports*, no. 32, Cairo 1981, pp. 1-21; Allen C. Kelley, Atef M. Khalifa and M. Nabil El-Khorazaty, *Population and Development in Rural Egypt*, Durham, North Carolina: Duke University Press, 1982, pp. 39-40 (hereafter: Kelley, Khalifa and El-Khorazaty).
13. *al-Ahram*, 6 August 1966.
14. *al-Jumhuriyya* (Cairo), 24 December 1965, 18 January 1966.
15. Ibid., 16 November 1965; *al-Ahram*, 26 March 1966.
16. Jumhuriyyat misr al-'arabiyya, al-jihaz al-markazi lil-ta'bi'a al-'amma wal-ihsa, *al-Kitab al-ihsa'i al-sanawi 1952-1980*, Cairo: al-Jihaz, 1982, p. 20.
17. WB, *World Tables* [1983], 3rd ed., vol. 2 — *Social Data*, Baltimore and London: Johns Hopkins University Press, 1984, p. 28.
18. CAPMAS, *SY 1985*, p. 3.
19. Nader Fergany, "The Development of National Population and Family Planning Policy in Egypt," UN, Economic Commission for Western Asia, First Regional Population Conference, Beirut, 1974, pp. 1-5; J. Mayone Stycos, Hussein Abdel Aziz Sayed, Roger Avery and Samuel Fridman, *Community Development and Family Planning: An Egyptian Experiment*, Boulder, Colorado: Westview Press, 1988; Hussein A. Sayed and Zeinab H. Amin, "An Evaluation of the Impact of the Population and Development Project, Based on Data from the 1984 Contraceptive Prevalence Survey," *Studies in African and Asian Demography, 1989*, Cairo Demographic Centre, *Research Monograph Series*, no. 19 (1990), pp. 444-47.
20. Israel Altman, "Islamic Movements in Egypt," *The Jerusalem Quarterly* 10 (1979): 87-105.
21. UNCTAD, *Handbook of International Trade and Development Statistics*, Supplement 1986, New York: UN, 1987, p. 426, table 6.2.
22. CAPMAS, *SY 1992*, p. 26, table 1-16.
23. WB, *World Tables 1989-90*, pp. 226-27.

24. *al-Ahram*, 24 January 1985. See also ESCWA, *Population Situation 1990*, p. 69.
25. *al-Ahram*, 1 May 1987, 21 July 1988, 2 May 1989, 1 May, 23 July 1990; *al-Musawwar*, 24 July 1992.
26. See, e.g., *al-Ahram*, 14, 21 April 1991, 27 September 1992.
27. Ibid., 20 July, 12 September 1988, 2 February 1989, 20 April, 6 May 1990.
28. See, e.g., *al-Ahram al-Iqtisadi*, 6 July 1992.
29. *al-Ahram*, 19 March, 17 November 1991; cf. id., 11 December 1990.
30. See, e.g., ibid., 26 February 1982.
31. See, e.g., ibid., 10 March, 10 September 1988, 24 January, 17 September 1989, 1 February 1990. See below, pp. 122–25, illustrations 7.1–7.6.
32. Ibid., 23 March 1991.
33. Ibid., 17 November 1991.
34. Barbara Entwisle, Linda J. Piccinino and Hussein Abdel Aziz Sayed, "Components of Family Planning in Rural Egypt," Cairo Demographic Centre, *Working Paper*, no. 15 (1988), p. 11 (hereafter: Entwisle, Piccinino and Sayed).
35. Ibid., pp. 9–10.
36. *al-Ahram al-Iqtisadi*, 9 July 1990.
37. Ibid., 22 July 1991.
38. Ibid., 26 August 1991.
39. *al-Ahram*, 8 March 1991, 11 May 1992.
40. Ibid., 26 August 1991.
41. CAPMAS, *SY 1988*, p. 6.
42. Entwisle, Piccinino and Sayed, p. 9.
43. Hussein Abdel Aziz Sayed, "Services Availability and Family Planning in Egypt," Cairo Demographic Centre, *Working Paper*, no. 24 (1991), p. 27.
44. Ibid., p. 44.
45. Ibid., p. 28, table 14.
46. Ibid., p. 46.
47. Ibid.
48. *al-Ahram*, 8, 27 March, 10 July 1991, 24 April 1992.
49. USAID, *Strengthening Egypt's Population Program*, Cairo: al-Mustaqbal, 1992, p. 34 (hereafter: USAID, *Egypt's Population*).
50. *Egyptian Gazette*, 1 November 1985, 19 December 1986, 13 July, 30 August 1987.
51. *al-Ahram al-Iqtisadi*, 26 February 1990.
52. *al-Musawwar*, 29 July 1988; *al-Jumhuriyya* (Cairo), 4 May 1989.
53. *al-Ahram*, 13 October 1987.
54. Ibid., 14 June 1990.
55. Mohamed S. Al-Dakkak, "The Interaction between the Legislative Policy and the Population Problem in Egypt," *Population Bulletin of ESCWA*, no. 30 (1987), p. 92 (hereafter: al-Dakkak).
56. *al-Ahram*, 12 May 1989. Cf. al-Dakkak, p. 88.
57. Hussein Abdel Aziz Sayed, "Preliminary Estimates of Some Demographic Measures for Egypt Based on Recent Sources of Data," *Studies in African and Asian Demography, 1989*, Cairo Demographic Centre, *Research Monographic Series*, no. 19 (1990), pp. 136, 138, table 16. Cf. Emma Tucker, "Fewer Children Mean a Better Life," *Financial Times*, 22 April 1993.
58. al-Dakkak, p. 88.
59. *al-Ahram*, 13 March 1987.
60. Nora L. Guhl, "Children's Patterns of Work in Egypt: Evidence from the Literacy and Numeracy Retention Study," *Studies in African and Asian Demography, 1989*, Cairo Demographic Centre, *Research Monograph Series*, no. 19 (1990), pp. 368–69 (hereafter: Guhl).
61. al-Dakkak, p. 93.
62. USAID, *Egypt's Population*, p. 34.
63. Ibid.
64. Ibid., p. 35.

65. Ibid.
66. CAPMAS, *SY 1992*, p. 243, table 11-9.
67. WB, *World Development Report 1991*, p. 224, table 11.
68. *al-Liwa al-Islami*, 19 December 1985; *Liwa al-Islam*, 26 April 1990.
69. *Liwa al-Islam*, 26 April 1990.
70. *al-Wafd*, 28 September 1988.
71. *al-Liwa al-Islami*, 26 December 1985, 8 October 1987, 25 May 1989, 8 March 1990.
72. *Liwa al-Islam*, 1 November 1989.
73. Wedad Zenie-Ziegler, *In Search of Shadows. Conversations with Egyptian Women*, London: Zed Books, 1988, pp. 37, 75.
74. Guhl, pp. 358-69.
75. Kelley, Khalifa and El-Khorazaty, pp. 8-12, 23-36.
76. *al-Ahram*, 5 October 1992.
77. Ibid., 15 May 1991, 24 April 1992; WB, *World Development Report 1992*, p. 270, table 27. Cf. MTM, 18 December 1992.

Index

137

141